THE IRISH STRUGGLE
1916–1926

Chapters by

F. X. Martin
Francis MacManus
Desmond Ryan
Patrick Lynch
G. A. Hayes-McCoy
Kevin B. Nowlan
Maureen Wall
F. S. L. Lyons
Frank Pakenham
Desmond Williams
Nicholas Mansergh
C. L. Mowat
Brian Ó Cuív
Richard Hawkins
Desmond Williams

THE IRISH STRUGGLE
1916–1926

Edited by
DESMOND WILLIAMS

University of Toronto Press

TORONTO

Published in Canada 1966
by University of Toronto Press

© *Routledge & Kegan Paul Ltd 1966*

Printed in Great Britain

CONTENTS

PREFACE

This book of fifteen essays in co-operative scholarship deals with a most contentious period of modern Irish history, that is, with the period between the Easter Rising of 1916 and the first years of the new Irish Free State government. It is a pioneering work in that it is the first book to deal intensively and from many viewpoints with a decade that included the Irish war for independence, the efforts of Irish and British leaders to arrive at a satisfactory settlement, the intricate Treaty negotiations, and the tragic civil war and its long bitter aftermath. The ideologies of the period are confused though the ideals are often simple and commanding.

Co-operative scholarship in history is not without its disadvantages, as the editor of the series, Professor Desmond Williams, well knows. There is some overlapping and repetition, necessary results of the genesis of the essays. Like a companion volume, *The Shaping of Modern Ireland*, this book had the same origins: it began as a series of lectures broadcast by Radio Éireann in 1963 and 1964 under the general title of the Thomas Davis Lectures, named in honour of the Irish nationalist thinker who declared 'Educate that you may be free'. For more than a dozen years, Thomas Davis lectures have been broadcast every autumn and winter and, as the radio officer immediately concerned, I have had the good fortune to work with the scholars.

Some of the lectures here presented were slightly altered; others were somewhat rewritten, added to and amended.

FRANCIS MacManus

vii

I

THE ORIGINS OF
THE IRISH RISING OF 1916

By Rev. F. X. Martin, O.S.A.

IRELAND HAD AS ITS FIRST HERO an Ulsterman, the legendary Cú Chulainn, leader and'pride of the Red Branch Knights. He became a symbol of Ireland's pre-christian virtues. The oldest Gaelic epic story, *Táin Bó Cualnge*, has left an unforgettable picture of his last fight. Queen Maebh of Connacht had sent an invincible army, 'the fighting men of the four fifths of Ireland' to overwhelm the province of Ulster. The Red Branch Knights fought with superhuman bravery in seven great battles until they were cut down to the last man. Laeg, the charioteer and inseparable companion of Cú Chulainn, fell beside his master, pierced by a spear. Only Cú Chulainn, the Hound of Ulster, remained, fatally wounded, his side and stomach gaping with wounds. He bound himself with his sword-belt to a pillar-stone, *Carrig-an-Compán*, so that he might die standing, facing his enemies. And so he did, with drawn sword in hand, a raven perched on his shoulder, the rays of the setting sun bright on his bronze helmet, a terror even in death to his enemies.

When Padraig Pearse founded St Enda's College at Cullenswood House in 1908 he had a saying of Cú Chulainn emblazoned around a fresco where all the boys might see it—'I care not though I were to live but one day and one night, if only my fame and my deeds live after me'. That was Pearse himself speaking through the mouth of Cú Chulainn. Again and again

Pearse reminded the boys of the heroic example set for them
by this Achilles of Ireland, the man who fought against
impossible odds. It was fitting, therefore, that in 1936 when a
monument in bronze was erected in the G.P.O. to the men of
1916 the figure chosen was the dying Cú Chulainn, standing
bound to the pillar-stone, with sword in hand.

The statue is meant to typify the indomitable spirit of the
Irish nation, and in particular of the men who fought in the
G.P.O. It is also an unintentional reminder of those forces
which prepared the way for the rising of Easter Week. Cú
Chulainn was the Hound of Ulster, and on reflection we shall
see that it was Ulster which played the decisive part in the
events leading to 1916.

When Pearse stood, pale-faced, in his grey-green uniform
outside the G.P.O. on Easter Monday, and read aloud the
proclamation of the republic to a small gathering of bewildered
bystanders he included an explanation for the revolt. He
mentioned the various military bodies—the I.R.B., the Irish
Volunteers, and the Irish Citizen Army—that had combined
for this armed effort against British control of the country. The
proclamation was not meant to be a full explanation of what
was taking place. It did not refer to some of the most important
forces and events which made 1916 possible.

Mahaffy, the brilliant anti-national provost of Trinity
College, Dublin, used to say that in Ireland the inevitable never
happens, the unexpected always. To an outsider looking at
Ireland in 1916 the rising came like a thunder clap from a blue
sky, and to the average Britisher it came at this crucial juncture
of the First World War as a stab in the back from an ungrateful
people. The rising was unexpected not merely in London but
in Dublin. On Easter Monday 1916 the average Dubliner was
thinking in terms of the Fairyhouse Races not of an armed
revolt. Even the very efficient British Intelligence Service in
Ireland was not aware of what was afoot. We have a copy of
the confidential report on the state of Ireland, written at the
request of the British authorities in April 1916, by Major Ivor
Price, Director of Military Intelligence in Ireland. Bear in mind
that the report is dated April 10, precisely a fortnight before the

rising. The document begins with the emphatic statements, 'The general state of Ireland, apart from recruiting, and apart from the activities of the pro-German Sinn Féin minority, is thoroughly satisfactory. The mass of the people are sound and loyal as regards the war, and the country is in a very prosperous state and very free from ordinary crime'.

It was inaccurate for Major Price to describe all the advanced Nationalists as of the Sinn Féin Party, but it would be true at that time to measure the vitality of the national spirit by the success or decline of the Sinn Féin group led by Arthur Griffith. What was the Sinn Féin story for these years? In 1908 Sinn Féin decided to make its first major appearance on the national stage, and to challenge in Ireland the supremacy of the Irish Parliamentary Party led by John Redmond in the British House of Commons. A Sinn Féin candidate, Charles Dolan, stood for a by-election in north county Leitrim. Dolan was a popular local man, who up to that time had sat as an Irish Parliamentary M.P. for this constituency. If Sinn Féin had any appeal in Ireland it would be shown to advantage in his case. Griffith and his supporters conducted an intense campaign in county Leitrim amid bitter opposition from John Redmond's followers. The result of the election was a flat rejection of Sinn Féin. Dolan received 1,157 votes as against 3,103 for the Irish Parliamentary Party candidate. Sinn Féin did not dare to enter the lists again for a further ten years.

But see what happened at the general election of December 1918. The Irish Parliamentary Party, which had held eighty seats in the House of Commons, was for all practical purposes swept out of existence; a mere seven of their candidates were returned as against seventy-three for Sinn Féin. This startling change in the fortunes of Sinn Féin was not the result of a gradual improvement between the years 1908 and 1918. The prospects for Sinn Féin early in 1916 seemed hardly any better than they had been in 1908. This we know from the confidential report, already mentioned, on the state of Ireland, written in April 1916 by Major Price, and based on the exact information sent to him by the R.I.C. who acted as the eyes and ears of the British Government throughout the country. One of the strongest indications that Pearse and the revolutionaries were in a decided minority and in desperate straits is that they had recourse to the bullet and not to the ballot.

It was obvious from the general election of 1918 that it was the execution of the 1916 leaders, and more particularly the threat of national conscription in 1918, which had caused a revulsion of popular feeling throughout most of Ireland. The Sinn Féin Party from being a nonentity became in a remarkably short time the strongest political organization in the country. Yet it is equally clear that this could not have happened unless the country as a whole was already predisposed by the time of the rising, certainly by 1918, for a sharp break with England. Who were the persons, and what were the factors, that prepared the country for this political somersault? That is the question to which we are seeking an answer. We are considering not 1916 and 1918, but their background.

Undoubtedly the Gaelic League was the greatest single force in propagating the separatist ideal among the Irish people during the twenty years before the rising. In February 1914 Pearse wrote as follows: 'The Gaelic League will be recognized in history as the most revolutionary influence that has ever come into Ireland. The Irish Revolution really began when the seven proto-Gaelic Leaguers met in O Connell Street. . . . The germ of all future Irish history was in that back room.'

The League was founded at Dublin in 1893. During the first ten decisive years of its existence three of its members were mainly responsible for the impact which the League made in Ireland: Fr Eoghan O Growney of Maynooth College; Eoin MacNeill, an official in the law courts at Dublin; Douglas Hyde, a graduate of Trinity College, Dublin. Of the three MacNeill contributed most to the success of the movement. O Growney's name became a household word throughout Ireland because of his grammar, entitled *Simple Lessons in Irish*, the key for unlocking the intricacies of the half-forgotten Irish language. It is not generally known that MacNeill helped substantially to prepare three out of the five parts for publication, and he alone was responsible for parts four and five.

Hyde became first president of the League, and held the

position for twenty-two years. He was an admirable choice; the League was non-political and undenominational; Hyde was a Protestant and had little interest in politics. He carried added prestige as a graduate of Trinity College and a scholar of some repute. But while he was given the centre of the stage, Eoin MacNeill, the undemonstrative young Ulsterman from the Glens of Antrim, was constantly in the background and the wings. It was an article by MacNeill in the March issue of the *Gaelic Journal* which called for a new organization to preserve Irish as a living language. He arranged the foundation meeting of the League, and asked Hyde to attend. MacNeill became its first secretary, unpaid, and for six critical years carried the burden of letter-writing and organizing. He was also editor of the *Gaelic Journal* from 1894 to 1899, and of *An Claidheamh Soluis* from 1899 to 1901.

The Gaelic League aroused a new spirit in the younger generation by means of its weekly classes, its publications, its summer colleges, the provincial *feiseanna*, the annual national *Oireachtas* and *Ard Fheis*, and the travelling organizers. The young people were swept along with enthusiasm as they delved deeper into what appeared to be the illimitable storehouse of wisdom and traditions in the Gaelic language and literature. The social effects of the League were profound. The youth of the country were provided with an Irish 'way of life', embracing their intellectual and recreational activities. The part played by women in the League was noteworthy, and coincided with the suffragette movement in England. The League gave women ample scope to exercise their gifts to further the national cause and to secure their own matrimonial ends. The importance of women in the national struggle became evident between the years 1916 to 1923.

Side by side with the Gaelic revival, and drawing inspiration from it, was the Anglo-Irish literary and dramatic movement, with figures such as Yeats, Lady Gregory, Synge, and Edward Martyn. Their influence on the events of 1916 and subsequently was indirect but real. It was not mere vanity which prompted Yeats to ask himself of his *Cathleen Ni Houlihan*:

> Did that play of mine send out
> Certain men the English shot?

This literary movement had its forerunner in Belfast, owing much to Alice Milligan and Eithne Carbery with their journal, the *Shan Van Vocht*. The dramatic movement was worthily represented in Belfast by the Ulster Theatre Group, their best-known production being perhaps the extravaganza, *Thompson in Tirnanoge*. During all this time the generous patron for the Irish-Ireland development in Ulster was Francis J. Bigger, whose house had an open door for anybody interested in the cultural revival. Among those drawn frequently to his house was the tall, bearded, strikingly handsome Roger Casement, home in county Antrim from his crusades in the Congo and Peru. His tragic story is one of the involved links between Ulster and 1916.

In discussing the origins of 1916 it may cause surprise that the Sinn Féin movement receives comparatively little notice. It has even been suggested that Sinn Féin changed its character after 1916. Certainly, the importance of Sinn Féin was after, not before, the rising. Yet, even before 1916 no political observer could disregard Arthur Griffith and his weekly newspaper, the *United Irishman*. He moulded a startling image of England before educated Irish eyes. Hitherto, English propagandists had, in newspapers and magazines, by means of cartoons and sketches, presented England as John Bull, that large, jovial, triumphant figure, with top hat, riding outfit, and a union jack for his waist-band. Griffith instead depicted him as a Frankenstein, a brutal master, who had, to use Griffith's own phrase, one hand on Ireland's throat and the other in Ireland's pocket. Griffith was proud of being Irish and a Dubliner, but in truth he was not typically Irish in name, character or appearance. He was not of native stock; his grandfather was an Ulster Presbyterian, a farmer in county Monaghan.

The later political fame of Griffith has tended to obscure the trojan task performed by D. P. Moran, another journalist of national importance. For thirty-six years Moran edited *The Leader*, of which he was also the proprietor. Its golden years were between 1900 and 1916. He set out with a lively and corrosive pen to abolish the 'stage Irishman', to kill bigotry, to

demolish the dominance of the Irish Parliamentary Party in
Ireland, to popularize Irish-made manufactures, to keep the
country Irish and Catholic, to make Ireland free and dignified.
Though good-natured by character he revelled in controversy
and barbed comments. He was a skilled journalist, trained in
London, responsible for putting into circulation words such as
seoinín, *ráméis*, and the like. He did not suffer fools gladly, be
they British imperialists or Gaelic star-gazers. He had a genius
for caustic nicknames—he christened George Russell (Æ) 'The
Hairy Fairy', and hostile Protestants 'Sourfaces'. He exalted
the ideal of an Irish Ireland, and yet he reduced the ideal to
practical terms of educational and economic progress. Altogether this sturdy square-jawed journalist served to hearten and
entertain the rising generation to a degree which is now
forgotten.

The part played in the national revival by the Gaelic Athletic
Association, better known as the G.A.A., was much more
effective than has been realized. The association was launched
at Thurles in November 1884, largely due to the exuberant
vigour of Michael Cusack and the powerful patronage of
Archbishop Croke. From the beginning Cusack and the co-
founders of the G.A.A. intended the association to be not just
another organization for sport but a means of forming a national
spirit. It was a separatist organization, explicitly hostile to
foreign games, backed privately by the republican groups
throughout the country. It spread with astonishing rapidity
from parish to parish, the length and breadth of Ireland. It has
been described as the first modern example of a national
democratic movement, supervised by local and county com-
mittees, under completely Irish auspices.

Whereas the studious and pensive were drawn to the Gaelic
League the athletic types sought a release for their energies in
the G.A.A. In fact many were members of both the G.A.A. and
the Gaelic League. Each G.A.A. club became a social focus
for the youth of an area. The Irish in England and Scotland
formed G.A.A. clubs, centres of Irish life in foreign surround-
ings. The political consequences of the clubs were plain. Many
of those who fought against the British in 1916 and from

1916 to 1922 were recruited from the G.A.A. During those troubled years when the carrying of arms was forbidden by the British authorities the public meetings of the republicans were often guarded by files of young men carrying hurleys, dangerous weapons in determined hands.

Even though the Gaelic League, the G.A.A. and the literary movement had aroused enthusiasm throughout the country for the ideal of an Irish Ireland there was no immediate prospect of a change in the political and social structure of the country. Arthur Griffith had an intense dedication to his object of a Sinn Féin Ireland, but he was a hard-headed idealist who looked to a vision not to a mirage. He stated quite bluntly that it would take two generations before Ireland would be educated to, and would accept, the Sinn Féin policy. The greatest obstacle he saw on the path to national self-determination was not England but John Redmond and his party. In the general election of 1910 the Irish Nationalists secured eighty-four seats out of 103; not merely had they an overwhelming majority of the Irish seats, but they held the balance of power in the House of Commons.

They represented the Catholic four-fifths of the population, but, Griffith and D. P. Moran pointedly asked, what real power did they wield in the country? The Viceregal Lodge remained the social magnet for the higher-middle and upper classes; Dublin Castle stood as the unchanging witness of England's administrative control of the country. In 1908 a French writer, Paul-Dubois, gave a revealing analysis of the balance of patronage: he stated, 'In the [Irish] Privy Council there are only seven Catholics as against fifty Protestants; of the eighteen judges in the High Court only three are Catholics; ... of the sixty-eight resident magistrates only nineteen are Catholics; of the county court judges only seven, of the thirty-seven county inspectors of police only four, and of the 124 district inspectors only from twenty to thirty.' He summed up, stating, 'Among the higher functionaries not more than one in five or six is a Catholic in religion or of nationalist sympathies in politics'.

The situation had been expressed with insolent candour by

Mahaffy of Trinity College, when he declared that 'it is a question not only of two creeds but of two breeds, of two ways of thinking, of two ways of looking at the most vital interests of men'. The Irish Catholics were still the lesser breed within the law. It was no accident then that it was the religious issue which overturned the political apple-cart. The scene of the crisis was Ulster, where religious passions still ran high. The Orangemen had their Catholic counterparts in the 'Molly Maguires' led by Joseph Devlin, the Nationalist M.P. for West Belfast. 'Wee Joe', as he was affectionately called by the Ulster Catholics, was not just a rabble-rouser; his abilities made him a principal lieutenant of John Redmond; in the House of Commons his size and oratory gained him the title of 'the pocket Demosthenes'.

As soon as it became known in 1911 that the prime minister, Asquith, intended to introduce a Home Rule Bill for Ireland the threatening rumble of Orange drums was heard across the northern province. The prospect of a parliament at Dublin, legislating for all Ireland but controlled by Redmond and his overwhelmingly Papist party, was more than Ulster Protestants could stomach. Once again the air became thick with the catch-cries of Parnellite days, 'Ulster will fight, and Ulster will be right', 'Home Rule is Rome Rule'. Left to themselves the Orange lodges might have ruined their own cause by premature violence or they might not have dared to spurn democracy by mounting a rebellion against their king and a civil war against their fellow-Irishmen. But they found an audacious leader in Ireland and powerful backing in England. Their Irish champion was Edward Carson, the Unionist M.P. for Trinity College. He had sternly represented law and order, when, dubbed 'Coercion Carson' by his critics, he held office as solicitor-general, first for Ireland, then for England. Now he gave his exceptional courage, experience and energies to armed defiance of lawful authority. Nor was he a lone rebel in high places. He and the Orangemen had the backing of the Conservative Party in England. The leader of the Conservatives was Bonar Law, Canadian-born but significantly enough, the son of an Ulster Presbyterian. The Conservatives saw the Ulster

B

crisis as a heaven-sent opportunity to topple Asquith and the Liberals from power.

According as the Home Rule Bill passed through its three readings in the British Parliament, Ulster moved steadily towards rebellion and civil war. The Ulster Volunteer Force was formed in November 1912, as the strong right arm of resistance to Home Rule; within little more than a year it numbered 100,000 volunteers. Money, officers and arms came from England, as did pledges of support from peers, generals and admirals. In September 1913 a 'provisional government of Ulster'—illegal of course—was formed at Belfast. Bonar Law, leader of the constitutional opposition in Parliament stated publicly at a monster meeting in Oxfordshire that the Ulster Volunteers would be justified in resisting Home Rule by all means in their power, including force. It was a Gilbertian situation: the supposedly unruly Nationalist Irish were placing their trust in law and order; the staid Conservatives were inciting a province of the empire to rebellion. Here, indeed, was what Asquith called 'the complete grammar of anarchy'.

The lesson of Ulster did not go unnoticed elsewhere in Ireland. Several Nationalists in Dublin had made up their minds that this was Ireland's hour of destiny, but it was Eoin MacNeill who sounded the call to arms. On November 1, 1913 the Gaelic League journal, *An Claidheamh Soluis*, published an article by MacNeill entitled 'The North Began'. He praised the Ulstermen for their courage, and suggested the formation of another volunteer corps throughout the rest of Ireland to demand fair terms for the country as a whole. Here was the opportunity for which the extreme Nationalists had been waiting. They wanted a leader above suspicion. MacNeill was an Ulsterman, a Catholic, a professor of the National University, with a nation-wide reputation as a man of patriotic but moderate political views. His appeal received an immediate response. He was visited by The O Rahilly and Bulmer Hobson, two men sworn to Irish independence. He assured them that he was prepared to lead also in action. The Volunteers were inaugurated at an overflow meeting in the Rotunda Rink on November 25, 1913. Anybody who was present that evening will vividly remember the electric silence as Eoin MacNeill rose to his feet on the platform, and announced in a ringing voice, 'Tosnuighimís anois, in ainm Dé!' ['Let us begin now, in the name of God!']. And begin they did: 4,000 men were enrolled on that occasion, and it was only the first wave of recruits.

Mention of Bulmer Hobson introduces the I.R.B., the most militant and persistent element in this movement for Irish independence. The I.R.B., Irish Republican Brotherhood or Fenians as they were called, had been a formidable threat to the British Government in Ireland during the 1860s, but by the end of the century they had gone into eclipse. They were content to meet as veterans rather than as active conspirators, to drink death to the British Empire and better days to Ireland. All this altered when a group of young Ulster patriots set about rejuvenating the organization. The change was due principally to two men, who are still alive—Denis McCullough and Bulmer Hobson. McCullough and Hobson first gained control of the Belfast I.R.B. circle, and insisted on sobriety and discipline. They did not hesitate to expel even close friends if they considered them unfit. Then, with the aid of Pat MacCartan they set about reviving the organization throughout Ulster, under the guise of the Dungannon Clubs. As their organizer they chose a young barman in Belfast, Sean MacDermott, the smiling rebel whose charm nobody could resist. They managed by dint of personal sacrifice and collections from friends to present MacDermott with a bicycle, and put him on the road at a salary of thirty shillings a week.

MacDermott in due time was transferred to Dublin, became a member of the Supreme Council of the I.R.B., and was (if anybody deserves the title) the mainspring of the rising in 1916. Hobson, a Quaker, tireless and dedicated to the goal of an Irish republic, also transferred to Dublin where he helped to infuse new life into the I.R.B. He was a member of the Supreme Council and editor of *Irish Freedom*, the I.R.B. newspaper. It was he who swore Pearse into the I.R.B. in December 1913, and organized the Howth gun-running in July 1914. He also, with Countess Markievicz founded the Fianna boy scouts who were to give a brave account of themselves in 1916. McCullough,

who had sworn MacDermott into the I.R.B., was president of
the Supreme Council at the time of the rising, and therefore,
first president of the Irish Republic proclaimed in 1916.[1]

The I.R.B. in Dublin gained a further stimulus when Tom
Clarke came to settle there in 1908. Clarke, though born in
England was reared at Dungannon, county Tyrone. He always
regarded himself as an Ulsterman. Because of his part in a
conspiracy to dynamite public buildings in England, he spent
fifteen galling years in English prisons. He had an unquench-
able desire to see an Irish Republic established by force of arms.
This small reticent man, with the piercing eyes, was neither a
notable organizer nor a persuasive orator, but for the younger

[1] Denis McCullough was unanimously elected president of the Supreme
Council at a meeting held in the Clontarf Town Hall in December 1915.
Pearse, Clarke and MacDermott were among those who voted. See L. N. Le
Roux, *Tom Clarke and the Irish Freedom Movement* (Dublin 1936), p. 176; D.
Lynch, *The I.R.B. and the 1916 Insurrection*, ed. F. O Donoghue (Cork 1957),
pp. 28–9.

The constitution of the I.R.B. then in force was the amended version of
1873; see P. S. O Hegarty, *A History of Ireland under the Union, 1801–1922*
(London 1952), pp. 414, 466.

Clause 11 of the constitution declared that the president of the Supreme
Council 'is in fact, as well as by right, president of the Irish Republic'.

The 1916 insurrection was organized by the Military Council of the
I.R.B. The seven members of the Military Council—Clarke, MacDermott,
Pearse, Connolly, MacDonagh, Kent and Plunkett—had taken an oath of
fidelity to the I.R.B. constitution. Clause 13 of the constitution stated that
the Military Council 'shall never be permitted to arrogate to itself the power
of legislating or restraining in any way the constitution of the Irish Republic
as promulgated by the Supreme Council'.

At the time of McCullough's election in December 1915 the decision to
launch the Rising had already been taken. Pearse and his comrades can
hardly have been unaware that in electing McCullough president of the
Supreme Council of the I.R.B. they were also conferring on him the
dangerous honour of being first president of the republic to be proclaimed
in 1916. It is significant that Pearse, in his dispatch from the G.P.O. dated
April 28, 1916, signs himself as president, not of the republic, but of the
provisional government of the republic; see dispatch in D. Ryan, *The Rising*
(Dublin 1957), pp. 144–5.

I am preparing a complete edition of the I.R.B. constitution for publication. An authentic version, containing the important clauses, numbers 11
and 13, is available in *Parnell Commission: Evidence, etc.*, IV (London 1890),
pp. 161–4.

members of the I.R.B. he was the incarnation of Ireland, militant, suffering, unbroken and unbreakable.

The other military force which accelerated the outbreak of the rising was the Irish Citizen Army. 'Army' is a grandiose term for a body which at the time of the rising mustered only 220 men; yet this company was determined to do battle, if necessary on its own, with the British Army in Dublin. It was almost an accident that the Citizen Army became involved in the rising. Jim Larkin and James Connolly, the two men who gave the Dublin workers the heart to arm themselves, thought in social rather than political terms. They were Socialists, Internationalists rather than Nationalists. The origin of the Citizen Army is not of the pattern of the other national movements.

In the early 1900s Dublin was notorious for its woefully inadequate wages and its disgraceful living conditions. More than one third of its people lived in one room tenements. Death and tuberculosis were highest in these single-room families; the death-rate percentage in Dublin was higher than Moscow with its rabbit-warren of slums and Calcutta with its teeming population and recurrent cholera. Dublin labourers worked a minimum of ten to twelve hours daily, usually at a weekly wage of eighteen to twenty shillings.

At the opportune hour 'Big Jim' Larkin burst on the Irish scene. This burly brass-throated orator was born in Liverpool of Ulster parents; they came from near Newry, driven by hunger to emigrate to England. 'Big Jim' was a boisterous fearless prophet of the gospel of social justice. He roused the Dublin workers to demand fair wages and he lashed the Dublin employers into a fury of retaliation. The Great Lock-Out of 1913 followed. It was an endurance test lasting eight months, and brought 100,000 workers and their dependents face to face with starvation or submission. Larkin summoned a public meeting to O Connell Street for Sunday, August 31, 1913, but it was banned by the British authorities. When Larkin audaciously eluded the police guard and appeared on the balcony of the Imperial Hotel the police in a frenzy of rage charged and savagely batoned the crowd, many of whom were passers-by or there from curiosity.

Four hundred civilians were treated for wounds. Blood calls for more blood. The Irish Citizen Army was formed under Captain J. R. White, a Protestant Ulsterman, the self-styled 'Misfit', an enthusiast for the freedom of Ireland and the rights of the working man. James Connolly, born in Scotland of Ulster parents, had been organizing the labour movement in Belfast. He settled at Dublin in October 1914, and henceforth under his guidance the Citizen Army became an offensive rather than a defensive body. While Pearse saw Ireland as *Cathleen Ni Houlihan* in chains, Connolly saw it as the working man in semi-starvation and squalor. For Connolly the British Government was both a foreign oppressor and an unscrupulous capitalist power. He became as determined as Pearse that Ireland should redeem its soul by a blood-sacrifice.

It is a sobering thought that despite the Gaelic League, the G.A.A., Sinn Féin, the Irish Volunteers, the I.R.B., and the Citizen Army, the mass of the Irish people early in 1916 were apparently, as Major Price commented, loyal to England. This seemed to be borne out by statistics: the maximum estimate of Irish Volunteers under the command of MacNeill and the Nationalists on the eve of the rising was 16,000, to which may be added 220 of the Citizen Army. By contrast there were 265,600 Irishmen serving either in the British Army or in allied British forces such as the R.I.C. Sixteen thousand as against 265,000 is a striking difference. Yet the statistics give a false impression: remember Mark Twain's remark, 'There are three kinds of lies—lies, damn lies and statistics'. Major Price misunderstood the situation when he stated that the mass of the Irish people were sound and loyal to England. They were loyal to John Redmond and the Irish Parliamentary Party. That loyalty was given because of the assurance that Redmond now had within his grasp the Home Rule concession for which O Connell, Butt and Parnell had unsuccessfully reached. The Home Rule Bill received the royal assent on September 18, 1914 and became law. Then, ironically, began the discrediting of Redmond and his party in the eyes of the Irish people.

There was already a growing doubt in Ireland about the sincerity and good intentions of the British government. There had been an epidemic of strikes in England and Belfast, but it was only at Dublin that the defenceless strikers and passers-by were brutally batoned by the police. The Ulster Volunteers openly defied lawful authority; they were aided and abetted by the Conservative Party and high-ranking military officials. But the Irish Volunteers were hampered and spied upon at every step. In March 1914 the so-called 'Mutiny at the Curragh' took place. Brigadier-General Hubert Gough and fifty-seven cavalry officers at the Curragh Camp announced that they would not move, if ordered, against Ulster. They were protected in parliament by the Conservatives, and had an Anglo-Irishman, Major-General Henry Wilson, as their secret adviser with the War Office. The fact that he was Director of Military Operations in the War Office did not deter him from political intrigue. In April 1914 the Ulster Volunteers ran a consignment of 20,000 rifles and 3,000,000 rounds of ammunition in at Larne, Bangor and Donaghadee; they transported it without interference for distribution throughout Ulster. Three months later Erskine Childers, after a hazardous voyage from the North Sea, skilfully ran his overloaded yacht, the *Asgard*, in at Howth with 900 rifles and 26,000 rounds of ammunition aboard. Awaiting the cargo on the quayside were columns of Irish Volunteers and Fianna boy scouts. Police and soldiers were mobilized to seize the arms but were outwitted. Some hours later a detachment of British troops marching back through the streets of Dublin were followed and jeered by the people at Bachelor's Walk. The soldiers fired on the crowd, killed three civilians and wounded thirty-five.

Was there one law for Ulster and another for the rest of Ireland? The situation had been epitomized during a scene in the House of Commons when an agitated Irish M.P. exclaimed to Balfour and the Conservatives, 'All I ask is justice for my poor country!' To which Balfour replied with languid arrogance, 'There isn't enough justice to go round'. In other words, Ireland which was hungering for justice would have to go at least half hungry. That principle became more evident after the outbreak of the European War in July 1914.

For a beginning the Home Rule Bill was declared suspended

until after the war; more ominous still, the government pledged that the bill would not come into force until an amending bill had been added about the temporary exclusion of Ulster. Nevertheless, Redmond threw himself enthusiastically into recruiting for England, as did Carson. But whereas the 29,000 Ulster Volunteers who joined the British Army were allowed to form a separate Ulster Division with their own officers and a distinctive badge, any similar privilege was denied to the 80,000 Irishmen who joined from the other three provinces. Redmond appealed again and again for a separate Irish Division, but in vain, even though Asquith had publicly promised that this would be done. The Secretary of State for War was an Anglo-Irishman, Kitchener. He had a near-contempt for Irish Nationalists and Catholics, and stood squarely by the Ulster Unionists.

A senseless rebuff was administered to the Irish Party when two prominent M.P.s, Stephen Gwynn and Willie Redmond, son of John, volunteered for the army but were refused commissions and had to join the ranks. The final straw was when Carson and J. H. Campbell, both of whom had incited the Ulstermen to armed rebellion, were called to high offices of state—Carson as a member of the British Coalition Cabinet, Campbell as Attorney-General for Ireland. Bishop Fogarty of Killaloe, hitherto a staunch supporter of the Irish Parliamentary Party, wrote bitterly to Redmond, 'Home Rule is dead and buried, and Ireland is without a national party or national press. What the future has in store for us God knows'.

Confidence in the Irish Parliamentary Party was undermined, and it needed only one final shock to complete the disillusionment of the Irish people. Pearse and the secret group of revolutionaries decided to ensure that this shock would be administered. They had little hope of military success, but were convinced that their blood-sacrifice would redeem Ireland. An armed rising would almost certainly provoke the British to harsh reprisals. This would prove that the government of Asquith was the same as that of Henry VIII, Elizabeth, Cromwell and William of Orange. They judged accurately. The Rising first puzzled and annoyed the Irish people; the executions which followed it shocked them. The Conscription Crisis of 1918 completed the process, and drove the moderates, even the clergy, to resist the government. The political vacuum created by the discrediting of the Irish Parliamentary Party was filled by Sinn Féin. Three provinces of Ireland were now on the road to rebellion.

Today outside the Northern Ireland House of Parliament at Stormont stands a massive statue of Carson, impressive in bronze as he was in the flesh, the Dublin lawyer who successfully led Ulster against the four-fifths of Ireland. The G.P.O. at Dublin has as its centre-piece the bronze statue of Cú Chulainn, the Hound of Ulster who fought to the last breath against the soldiers of the four-fifths of Ireland. The two statues express one of the paradoxes of Irish history. Ulster is both the cause of partition, and an unintentional major cause of the independence of the twenty-six counties. From that paradox each person may draw his own conclusions.

Select bibliography:

Greaves (Desmond), *Life and times of James Connolly*, London 1961.
Gwynn (Denis), *John Redmond*, London 1932.
Holt (Edgar), *Protest in Arms: the Irish Troubles, 1916-23*, London 1960.
Horgan (John), *Parnell to Pearse*, Dublin 1948.
Hyde (H. Montgomery), *Carson*, London 1953.
Le Roux (L. N.), *Tom Clarke and the Irish Freedom Movement*, Dublin 1936.
Martin (F. X.), 'Eoin MacNeill and the 1916 Rising', in *Irish Historical Studies*, 12 (1961) 226-271.
Martin (F. X.), ed. *The Irish Volunteers, 1913-1915*, Dublin 1963.
Martin (F. X.), ed. *The Howth Gun-Running, 1914*, Dublin 1964.
Ó Luing (Sean), *Art Ó Griofa*, Dublin 1953.
O'Brien (Conor Cruise), ed., *The shaping of modern Ireland, 1891-1916*, London 1960.
Pearse (P. H.), *Collected Writings, ed. D. Ryan*, 5 vols, Dublin, n.d. *Royal Commission on the Rebellion in Ireland*, London 1916.
Tierney (Michael), 'Eoin MacNeill: a biographical study', in *Eoin MacNeill, Saint Patrick*, ed. J. Ryan, Dublin 1964, pp. 9-34.

2

IMAGINATIVE LITERATURE AND THE REVOLUTION

By Francis MacManus

O N A SUNDAY NIGHT in October 1921, one of the most intelligent leaders of the guerrilla warfare being waged in Ireland against the British occupation forces, stood on the stage of the Abbey Theatre and told the audience: 'It seems to me that we have been deserted at the present time and all through the fight put up in the country by our poets and by our literary people.'

What the man of action wanted, of course, from the poets and the literary men, was propaganda for his cause and the expression of an ideology. The trouble was that while there was a cause there was no ideology and never had been. Pearse had tried to create one and what he had succeeded in expressing and teaching was an idealism, a set of ideas and a complex of emotions that amounted to a mystical act of faith in the living and historic Irish nation. Only in a series of intensive studies biographical as well as literary, could one hope to show adequately how the writers reacted in their individual ways, how they committed themselves or indeed moved aside from the rights and wrongs of the struggle. One thing the writers had in common who were not privy to the preparations for the rising: they, like most of the population and the British government in Dublin and London, were taken quite by surprise.

'This has taken every one by surprise', wrote James Stephens, then a clerk in a city office, in the first lines of the journal which he set down as starting on Easter Monday and later published as *The Insurrection in Dublin*. On that morning, as he said, 'I awoke into full insurrection and bloody war, but I did not know anything about it'. He was quickly to learn much about it and in his narrative he created a queer sharp clarity in which civilians and fighters, conversations and shootings, occur with the sort of preternaturally vivid ordinariness that invests nightmares. His book was more than good reporting. Stephens was sympathetic. He tried to understand.

While these things were happening, W. B. Yeats was staying with the Rothensteins in England. He, too, was surprised. Although he knew some of the leaders he had not been a party to the counsels of the new generation of Nationalists. To Rothenstein he spoke about innocent and patriotic theorists who were carried away by the belief that they must sacrifice themselves to an abstraction. To Lady Gregory he wrote about the 'heroic, tragic lunacy of Sinn Féin'. But his feelings were already engaged to such an intensity that never during the following decade would they be free of entanglement in the struggle, though they might be ambivalent. The executions were taking place when again he wrote to Lady Gregory to doubt 'that justice is being worked with precision in Dublin'. He was then, he said, trying to write a poem about the men executed and the words 'terrible beauty has been born again' were forming themselves as a key-phrase. Within a few weeks he had completed his poem, *Easter 1916*. It was printed in an edition of twenty-five copies 'for distribution amongst friends' and other poems followed but they were withheld from the general public until 1920. That he was prudent or cautious in the publication of these poems is probably not unconnected with the intensity and depth of the effect of the rising on him. Something new was born, or rather something old was revived in Yeats. Just three years before when he wrote about romantic Ireland being dead and gone—'It's with O'Leary in the grave' —he had described Ireland as becoming 'a little greasy huxtering nation groping for halfpence in a greasy till'. And then suddenly, there was the fire blazing in Dublin and men being shot for having fought—men he had known who were now transfigured:

> Was it needless death after all?
> For England may keep faith
> For all that is done and said.
> We know their dream; enough
> To know they dreamed and are dead;
> And what if excess of love
> Bewildered them till they died?
> I write it out in a verse—
> MacDonagh and MacBride
> And Connolly and Pearse
> Now and in time to be,
> Wherever green is worn,
> Are changed, changed utterly:
> A terrible beauty is born.

Repetition and reproduction have made the poem—and others of the time—hackneyed; but Yeats's intuition about the birth of 'a terrible beauty' was shared by other poets who also saw the terribleness as well as the beauty. Æ could write that the leaders' dream had left him numb and cold but his spirit had risen in pride:

> Here's to you, Pearse, your dream, not mine.
> But yet the thought, for this you died,
> Has turned life's water into wine.

One of the ideals held by Pearse, by the pupils of his school in Rathfarnham, and by other leaders including members of the Gaelic League, was the creation of a Gaelic-speaking Ireland. But what was the immediate effect of the rising on Gaelic writing? Only one book worth mentioning in this regard appeared in that decade after Easter Week. It was a collection of seven short stories by Padraic O Conaire, published in 1918 under the title *Seacht mBuaidh an Eirghe Amach* which might be translated as *Seven Victories of the Rising*. The book became very popular and by the end of the 'Twenties it would be used in colleges and schools as a classic and so help to form an unbalanced reputation for the author. What O Conaire did in the seven stories was, to give a few instances, to show how 'the terrible beauty' affected the illegitimate son of the heir to a Big House; two women who hide from each other the death in the rising of a man they both love; a bishop who has to deal with a young priest who sides with the rebels; and a romantic poet who betrays a woman. This last is like a poor Maupassant story rewritten by, say, Ethel M. Dell. Indeed, the emotion in some of the stories tends to become sentimental and the writing gushy.

The stories were more of a gloss on 'a terrible beauty is born' rather than an imaginative re-creation of how and why the rising had come about and how it had affected various levels of Irish society. Such a re-creation was to come in the bulky, ambitious and somewhat dull novel, *The Wasted Island* by Eimar O'Duffy. This novel was finished in Dublin, in October 1919. It is the most comprehensive essay in fiction about the rising ever attempted. It studies the self-sacrificing patriotism and the 'greasy till' conservatism that were the life-spark and the matrix of the rising. It is didactic, loquacious, ramshackle in structure, but always sincere and probably autobiographical to a large extent. Bernard Lascelles, one of the two focal figures of the novel, is perhaps nearest to O'Duffy himself in class, upbringing and experience. He is the son of a snobbish, class-conscious, pro-British Protestant Dublin surgeon and the rather stupid affectionate Catholic, Alice Reilly. It is through Alice Reilly's brother, a Nationalist, that Bernard is made conscious of Ireland's history and legendary past. The other focal figure is another young man, Stephen Ward, who is raised in isolation on frugal fare and high thinking in a cottage in the Dublin mountains by a disillusioned Fenian father who is determined that his son will not make a fool of himself for the sake of Ireland. Both father and son, are not, to use Anthony Trollope's definition of the novelist's task, human figures in whom one is forced to believe.

The lives of the two young men run side by side, touch, intertwine and provide the viewpoints for the comprehensive survey of Irish life which is one of the novel's virtues. Through their eyes and minds we are given Dublin society from the level of the stuffy ruling and stuffier professional class down to the delirious squalor of the slums. The novel is full of hours and hours of talk and of arguments that are, for all their point and wit, like formal debates. It is plain that the author, Eimar O'Duffy, was trying to work out for himself a philosophy that would encompass both the high mystical patriotism of the Pearse-Plunkett group and the social struggle of the working class who had endured the crisis, starvation and the police batons in 1913.

By the time O'Duffy's novel appeared, guerilla warfare—raids, ambushes, reprisal killings, burnings and arrests were creating a wasted island: in Lady Gregory's phrase, 'Death answering to Death like the clerks answering one another at the Mass'. In that year, Yeats chose to publish his verse play, *The Dreaming of the Bones*, in which the verse is more like music than dialogue. A young volunteer escapes from the Post Office in Dublin after the rising and meets in county Clare the ghosts

> of Diarmuid and Dervorgilla
> Who brought the Norman in.

The pair wander in an endless purgatory of separation and of unconsummated love but

> If someone of their race forgave at last
> Lip would be pressed on lip.

The young man says with fearful intensity:

> O, never never
> Shall Diarmuid and Dervorgilla be forgiven.

Yeats himself thought the play politically strong. It was strong in its expression of intransigent hatred but it was too mannered, too aloof. He was not, of course, so naive as to believe that Irish grievances were based on an invasion seven centuries old. There was fuel enough for raging fire in what was then happening. One stanza from the sequence of poems entitled *Nineteen Hundred and Nineteen* provides a key to the effect on his mind of the violence into which hatred had exploded:

Now days are dragon-ridden, the nightmare
Rides upon sleep: a drunken soldiery
Can leave the mother, murdered at her door,
The night can sweat with terror as before
We pieced our thoughts into philosophy,
And planned to bring the world under a rule,
Who are but weasels fighting in a hole.

So, we have the somewhat detached but deeply disturbed
Yeats; O'Duffy committed emotionally but remaining critical;
O Conaire believing but yet humorous, satirical and a bit
pessimistic. Was there no writer of the time who gave himself
fully to the revolution?

There was. He was the Cork writer, Daniel Corkery, a most
gifted contemplative and critical scholarly man, well-read in
the literatures of Europe including the great Russians, and a
passionate believer in the Gaelic tradition which, so to speak,
was the marrow of his bones. In later years, two of his most
brilliant literary disciples, Frank O'Connor and Sean O'Faolain,
would use the revolution in which they took an active part as
material for the very impressive short stories that would earn
them both international reputations. In 1920, Daniel Corkery
published ten short stories about the Irish war for independence
under the historico-romantic title, *The Hounds of Banba*. Long
out of print, these stories are more than propaganda on a party
line. As Ernest Boyd said in his history of the Irish literary
renascence, 'Here is the conflict of two races and two civiliza-
tions, not in terms of politics, but in terms of humanity'. Those
were the terms in which this Corkman wrote, and three of the
stories are among his best—*The Ember, Cowards* and *Colonel
MacGillicuddy Goes Home*. They are, perhaps, limited in their
universal appeal by two factors. One is their very historicity.
The conditions of the armed revolution are faithfully recorded.
The other is that the men with the guns seem to have borrowed
something from the committed and contemplative mind of the
author like, to quote Benedict Kiely, 'a singing procession of
fighting men silent for a few moments as they march in the
shadow of a convent wall'.

Corkery may have been a romantic about peasants but he

adhered to the modesty of nature. He knew terrible things were being done and he knew that the fighting had an economic and cultural impulse as well as a political. But he never doubted the cause, never came to reject the war as a fight between weasels in a hole. He is completely engaged. His figures are, as he is, obsessed by tradition and history. They fight not merely for the living but for the dead. 'I saw', he wrote, 'that every extreme movement in Ireland leaves behind it a remnant of its broken army, an old workman in a factory in a city, a cobbler in a little shop in a village, or . . . a shepherd in a hut on a mountainside—great old hearts that preserve to the next generation, even to the second next, the spark of fire that they themselves had received in the self-same manner from those that long since were gone home into the silence'.

The quotation is not untypical. Such a phrase as 'gone home into the silence' reveals the literary romanticism of Corkery's approach. But—to jump five years ahead for a comparison with Liam O'Flaherty's *The Informer*—his narratives of the guerilla war possess the dignity of a people who were unvanquished. *The Informer* has been a more widely read, more successful book but it is romantic melodrama, a peg to hang a man on, against a grim and sordid Dublin background which is no more than a background. The people are puppets jerked and tossed about in a *danse macabre* in a story of almost animal violence. The speech is synthetic. The revolutionary organization in the story is Communist and militant, more like something out of a bad German or Polish novel. Gypo Nolan, the informer, is a sort of primeval Judas, more ape than man, and although he has been able to serve as an altar-boy and work as a policeman—the old R.I.C. were not geniuses but they were disciplined and trained—he is presented as a brutal troglodyte, in whose brain just two facts can make what the author calls 'that loud primeval noise which is the beginning of thought'. Yet Yeats considered this—and *Mr. Gilhooley*—a great novel, 'too full of abounding life to be terrible despite the subjects'.

Yeats himself was shuttling between England and Ireland, and between Dublin and the old tower of Ballylee in county Galway. In Dublin he looked after, among other things, the

C

Abbey Theatre which would yet bring forth the greatest drama of the revolution. In that old tower he could sit in a rather chilly room above the chattering trout stream and meditate on the things that were his passion and look down to see signs of a world now in civil war—cars carrying coffins; marching men; smoke from a burning house. It was here he wrote his most impressive but difficult suite of seven poems entitled *Meditations in Time of Civil War*—a pondering of the perennial nightmare of violence in relation to the philosophic life. His fears, his profound perturbation and his desire for creative peace, are most clearly stated in the poem about the starling's nest by his window:

> The bees build in the crevices
> Of loosening masonry, and there
> The mother birds bring grubs and flies.
> My wall is loosening; honey-bees,
> Come build in the empty house of the stare.
>
> We are closed in, and the key is turned
> On our uncertainty; somewhere
> A man is killed, or a house burned,
> Yet no clear fact to be discerned:
> Come build in the empty house of the stare;
>
> A barricade of stone or of wood;
> Some fourteen days of civil war;
> Last night they trundled down the road
> That dead young soldier in his blood;
> Come build in the empty house of the stare.
>
> We had fed the heart on fantasies,
> The heart's grown brutal from the fare;
> More substance in our enmities
> Than in our love; O honey-bees,
> Come build in the empty house of the stare.

Was it true that hearts had fed on fantasies during all those years of war since the rising, and that there was now more substance in enmities than in love? Perhaps not even the most intensive histories could answer the questions. There were some who, like Yeats himself, hungered and thirsted for an end on some sort of terms. Others thought like Frank Gallagher, author of a journal kept in prison on hunger-strike and later published as *Days of Fear*. Lady Gregory believed it would be one of the great books of the world and it is quite likely she was sympathetic to Gallagher's reasons for being against the Treaty. He wanted to keep republicanism alive because otherwise the young men might lose this idea of freedom, the most spiritual thing they had ever attained, for mere industrial and material undertakings. Such idealism would have tasted like a mouthful of ashes to a man who was late in starting his career as a dramatist. Sean O'Casey was in his forties before the Irish public through the Abbey Theatre got a taste, and then two large draughts of his genius. In his autobiography in years to come Yeats's famous line would run:

> A terrible beauty is borneo,
> Republicans once so forlorneo,
> Subjected to all kinds of scorneo.

However, something much more than a mocker of the heroic principle had come. O'Casey was a Nationalist but by experience and observation, as well as by his reading in socialist writings, he became a disillusioned idealist. In 1923, O'Casey sent the fourth play he had written to the Abbey. It was about the Black-and-Tan war and the title, *On the Run*, became *The Shadow of a Gunman*. He had discovered his Dublin idiom and that bitter mixture of tragedy, comedy and farce which was also to be the receipt for the two great plays that followed. *The Gunman* is about the hero as an illusionist who brings death with his fantasies. Minnie Powell, the slum girl in the play, dies because he is a fake-poet and poltroon. She dies for the heroism he does not possess. The pedlar, Seamus Shields, dodges bullets, is candidly afraid, and wishes to God it was all over. In a shrewd protesting passage about how war, bombs, guns and killings, have become a religion, he says:

> It's the civilians who suffer; when there's an ambush, they don't know where to run. Shot in the back to save the British Empire, an' shot in the breast to save the soul of Ireland.

And later, he says something which does indicate what was O'Casey's attitude:

> I believe in the freedom of Ireland, an' that England has no right to be here, but I draw the line when I hear the gunmen blowin' about dyin' for the people, when it's the people that are dyin' for the gunmen!

On March 3, 1924, *Juno and the Paycock* had its first night at the Abbey Theatre and at least two characters, 'Captain' Boyle and 'Joxer' Daly stepped across the footlights out of this tragedy of civil war to join the characters that are at large, as it were, from the great plays of the world. Lady Gregory wrote in her journal:

> A wonderful and terrible play of futility, of irony, humour, tragedy.

And, one might add—a play of the delirium that can afflict the human condition. In the last crazy drunken scene 'Captain' Boyle drools out the famous words:

> I'm telling you . . . Joxer . . . the whole worl's in a terr . . . ible state o' . . . chassis!

Only a few minutes previously Juno Boyle had protested and prayed as other women had protested or prayed—Minnie Powell in *The Shadow of a Gunman* or Bessie Burgess in *The Plough and the Stars*, which was to be the third of the three great plays about the decade: Mrs Boyle had said:

> Mother o' God, Mother o' God, have pity on us all! Blessed Virgin, where were you when me darlin' son was riddled with bullets? Sacred Heart o' Jesus, take away our hearts o' stone, and give us hearts o' flesh! Take away this murdherin' hate, and give us Thine own eternal love!

It is a matter of history—a footnote, perhaps for curious posterity—that when *The Plough and the Stars* was produced a year later, there was trouble with some of the Abbey players who objected to certain lines, trouble with one of the directors, and then with the audience who rioted while Yeats tried to make a speech. Romantic Ireland was not, indeed, dead and gone. It was there, in the audience, among the critics and even among some of the writers who protested against O'Casey's feverish vision of reality. The old idealism hadn't succumbed during the years of guerrilla and civil war. A mythopoeic process was at work on the rising, the leaders, their utterances and lives. They would become so sanctified, if one may use the word, that their deep humanity, the very ground of their heroism, would signify less than the images fashioned of them; and even those images would fade, too, as the century rolled on and they received a deference that would become more and more ritualized. But the humanity and the agonies of the Dublin in which they had risen would be held, with all the thrust of life, in those plays written by Sean O'Casey.

In her journal, the busy great-hearted woman, Lady Gregory wrote words that have the air of finality:

> An overpowering play. I felt at the end of it as if I should never care to look at another; all others would seem so shadowy to the mind after this.

Wasps, not honey-bees, had come to live in the house of the stare.

In September of that same year, 1926, the Abbey Theatre produced another play that had come out of the pain of those years of war. This was *The Big House* by the fine craftsman, Lennox Robinson. He tried to present the predicament of the Anglo-Irish, now no longer top dogs. Many of them had left the country, fled from burnt-out houses or threats or from what looked like the hopeless condition of colonials abandoned by England. Some of them stayed on. In his play, Robinson tried to be fair not only to those who were on his side of the colonial demesne wall but also to what the Irish struggle signified. And with what must have been at the time more like determined optimism than hope based on realities, he makes his heroine, a daughter of the Big House, say:

> I was wrong, we were all wrong, in trying to find a common platform, in pretending we weren't different from every Pat and Mick in the village. . . . We must glory in our difference, be as proud of it as they are of theirs. . . . Why, because we're what we are. Ireland is not more theirs than ours.

It is for historians of the later decades to tell how those whom Brendan Behan has called 'the Horse-Protestants' survived, took part in the affairs of the country even if only for the sake of horses, gloried less and less in their difference, and found 'them'—the mere Irish of history—peculiarly tolerant. But in those same decades, the vision that had lured the young men to fight in the streets of Dublin had suffered the attrition of the years.

3

SINN FÉIN POLICY
AND PRACTICE (1916–1926)

By Desmond Ryan

THERE WERE TIMES before the rising when Sinn Féin might quite plausibly and with some show of reason have been dismissed by its enemies as one of the greatest window-dressing myths in modern history, however evident its impact might have been on the public mind from its formal beginnings in the years after Parnell's death. But in the ruin and uproar which succeeded the year of Terrible Beauty, its enemies transformed it into the world force it has since proved itself to be: from Ireland to Cyprus, to India, to Africa and in all the anti-colonial struggles of today.

In the case of Sinn Féin, the result was the eventual triumph of an Irish Republic as Sinn Féin, transmuted into an irresistible force in which bloodshed, political assassination, guerrilla warfare and an underground half-functioning national assembly brought the foreign occupying power to a standstill and ultimate checkmate.

And yet its enemies might still maintain that Sinn Féin remained an aspiration, a facade, an Irish farce, with everything except the one essential: executive power. Indeed its founders had hardly hoped for anything more at most than the old dual monarchy of Grattan's days; hardly indeed for an Irish Republic, even though that ultimate ideal was there in Lalor's defiant phrase: 'The banner that floats nearest to the sky'. The result, too, had been achieved by violent methods which Arthur

31

Griffith, Edward Martyn, John Sweetman, Thomas Shine Cuffe, Alderman Tom Kelly, Walter Cole and the other founders of Sinn Féin had previously rejected for the near-pacifist methods of passive resistance: that is, non-payment of taxes, anti-recruiting campaigns, ceaseless propaganda, industrial and agricultural developments—and an Irish version of Deak's Hungarian battle of the 1840s against Austria.

Or as Griffith more specifically defined it, in 1904, in his 'Resurrection of Hungary'; 'From the inception of the *United Irishman*—(in 1899)—we have opposed the sending of Irishmen to sit in the British Parliament on two grounds. Firstly, that it is the recognition of the usurped authority of a foreign assembly to make laws to bind the people of Ireland, and secondly, that the policy of parliamentarianism has been materially and morally disastrous to the country. We need not labour the latter point. No measure of a beneficial nature has ever been passed by the British Parliament as a result of the presence, speeches and action of the delegation from Ireland. The five measures which are usually accepted as beneficial for Ireland passed by that Parliament: The Catholic Emancipation Act, the Tithes Act, the Church Disestablishment Act, the Land Act of 1881, and the Local Government Act, were passed as a result of the unconscious carrying-out by the people of the Hungarian policy—the policy of Passive Resistance—with occasional excursions into the domain of Active Resistance at strategic points. . . .'.

Griffith recalled to his readers the statesmanlike idea of O'Connell in his later life. This was to summon the Irish Parliament in Dublin, which to O'Connell was still the legal body. It was to be called the Council of Three Hundred, and its purpose was to legislate for the country, on the grounds that Grattan's Parliament was still the legal one, and that the new machinery of government should be exercised through O'Connell's own Repeal Clubs. But this body never met, and the English Government breathed freely again.

This proposal was then completely forgotten until two generations later, when the situation was briefly this: the public mind had been stirred by the Irish-Ireland movement with its emphasis on economic and cultural self-sufficiency, its optimism and its self-confidence. So that the contemporary impact of Sinn Féin was terrific, that is, to a far-seeing minority. This development was quickened by three events above all: the uprise of the armed Ulster Volunteer Movement, in itself a lively adaptation of that old Council of Three Hundred, secondly, the rioting and violence that marked the Dublin strike of 1913, and thirdly and chiefly, the outbreak of the European War in 1914. Within two years, on two occasions within the same week, Griffith took two contradictory and inconsistent positions on the rights and wrongs of the use of armed force. On April 22, 1916 Griffith vigorously supported Eoin MacNeill in his measures to countermand the Insurrection fixed for the next day. He took no part in the rising, but as the insurrection collapsed, he made his way again to consult and support MacNeill in a last-minute appeal for the country to rise and support the Dublin insurgents. This document was never circulated, as Pearse had already ordered an unconditional surrender. This is the solitary instance in his life of anything like a martial gesture. For the last six years of his life he felt himself obliged to follow the tide, a tide which led to guerrilla warfare. At heart Griffith deplored this. Publicly he maintained his reserve, but privately he unambiguously and categorically denounced it to such intimates and colleagues as Robert Brennan and P. S. O'Hegarty. He frowned on the Soloheadbeg Ambush of January 21, 1919, and the Bloody Sunday shootings of British Intelligence Officers in Dublin on November 21, 1920 appalled him. 'We cannot defend this' he said. His condemnation of the assassination of Sir Henry Wilson on June 22, 1922 was emphatic and public: 'It is a fundamental principle of civilized government that the assassination of a political opponent cannot be justified or condoned. . . . This is an anarchic deed.'

Not alone was the pacifist basis of Sinn Féin undermined after Easter Week, the constitutional programme imperatively called for re-definition. The sequel was the compromise set forth in the revised Constitution of Sinn Féin adopted at the Ard Fheis in 1917. It was based on the formula that Fintan

Lalor had given to the Repeal Clubs of the country and to the Confederates in the crisis of January 1848: 'No mode of connection between the kingdoms' (that is to say, the kingdoms of Great Britain and Ireland) 'could be solid, desirable or lasting except a "*Federal Union*", such as that existing between New York and Pennsylvania. But a Federal Union must be the result of *negotiation* and agreement between the negotiating parties . . . but in order to negotiate the parties must stand on equal terms, and each be *independent* of the other. *Independence*, therefore, full and entire independence is a necessary preliminary to any permanent or satisfactory arrangement with Britain. The steps are: independence, negotiation and Federal Union. . . .'

Lalor here postulated what is now a commonplace, but unrecognized in his own time, that is, the virtual independence of the member states of the future British Commonwealth. The two first points, Independence and Negotiation, are the planks of timber which Eamon de Valera in 1917 used to build a bridge for Sinn Féin across the gulf from theory to actuality in the years of transition then begun.

The amended Constitution of Sinn Féin in 1917 contains these most seminal clauses:

'Sinn Féin aims at securing the international recognition of Ireland as an independent Irish Republic.

Having achieved that status, the Irish people may by Referendum freely choose their own form of Government.'

This to Griffith meant Grattan's Parliament guaranteed in 1782, in a word, a dual-monarchy; to Cathal Brugha nothing less than an Irish Republic in name and in fact; to de Valera external association aptly defined in the London *Times* as 'an independent State essentially though not in name a Republic in loose association with the British Commonwealth'. The actuality was Griffith's old dream of a National Assembly. With this difference: it was backed by the support of a majority of the people as a sequel to a national revolution. If the Provisional Government of Ulster had been indeed a very militant caricature of that O'Connellite Council of Three Hundred, this indeed surpassed the tentative Sinn Féin plan of a decade

before, which had been based on the system of local government
bodies and financially supported by voluntary contributions.
From January 21, 1919, Dáil Éireann formally proclaimed that
the Government of the Irish Republic was based on universal
suffrage, and financially on funds subscribed by means of a
loan floated in Ireland and America, under a system of interest-
bearing Dáil Bonds. Within certain limits, the *de facto* government of Dáil Éireann backed by popular consent and supported
by its reserve of physical force, functioned. The limit, indeed,
was the superior physical force of Great Britain. This last
reduced Dáil Éireann's Civil Government, with three partial
exceptions, to ineffective window-dressing. The three exceptions
were real and effective enough. They were: The Dáil Bonds
just mentioned, the Secret Army, and that section of the civil
machinery which superseded British Police, Courts of Justice
the Dáil, arbitration tribunals which averted the deadly danger
of a class struggle in the Sinn Féin ranks. At the end of the five
years' struggle there was deadlock. The unequal guerrilla
struggle and such frenzied heroism as Terence MacSwiney's
fast to death could not avail to dislodge the overwhelming force
of Great Britain in occupation. This was the basic fact of the
whole situation, which not even the skilful propaganda of
Erskine Childers's subtle apologia, in his two anonymous
pamphlets: *The Constructive Work of Dáil Éireann* could obscure.
Even that master-propagandist more than once was driven
back by the very recital of facts to such a fatal admission as
'Meanwhile, the Republican Parliament and Government,
based on the rock of popular consent, functioned, and functioned effectively; not over the whole field of administration,
for that was physically impossible in the midst of a military
occupation; but up to the limit imposed by superior physical
force'. The admission is crucial. If the physical and spiritual
struggle maintained by the mass of the people was indeed
impressive and evident, even more evident was a large spicing
of humbug in such solemn pretences as Commissions of Enquiry
into the Resources and Industries of Ireland. Cultural triflings
of Fine Art Ministries came to nothing. The deadly tyranny of
a ruthless party machine blunted the moral basis of Dáil

Éireann's appeal to the nations of the world, if indeed in a time
of world war appeals to democracy, self-determination, rights
of small nations and all that could be taken seriously. This is a
hard saying. The Dáil's appeal to the world expressed all that
was great and lasting in the national case, yet armed force
overshadowed ideals and principles however loudly applauded.
Dáil Éireann was driven underground and its temporary
successes in such departments as police, lawcourts and land
arbitration nullified. A sympathetic and contemporary historian
of Sinn Féin, who played a dangerous and important part in
the struggle, candidly admitted that the Dáil Éireann social
and democratic programme did not represent anything more
than pious lip-service, and would not have been endorsed by
the deputies in any effective form. In short, patriotism was the
reality, social reform a dream of the future.

In actual fact, social reform was not such a dream of the
future. Even the British Government, through its more enlightened minds, had anticipated the inevitable collapse of the
landlord system. In 1903, a year before the foundation of Sinn
Féin, George Wyndham and a representative conference of
Nationalists and Unionists had taken the first decisive steps
towards the solution of the Irish Land Problem. This peaceful
revolution, begun with the Congested District Board and the
Land Commission, was only finally completed by Patrick
Hogan, William Cosgrave's Minister of Agriculture, in the
1920s. A decade later, a clause in the Chamberlain-de Valera
pact in 1937 put the crown on one of the most sweeping social
changes in Irish history. In a word, the settlement of the Land
Annuities issue which liquidated the five years' economic war,
1932 to 1937.

It was then, some fifteen years after his death, that the
historic significance of Sinn Féin and the stature of Arthur
Griffith as a leader and a statesman became clear, with one
tantalizing exception: Partition. The economic and political
ideals were working out to a consistent and successful climax.
As a leader from 1916 to 1922 Griffith justified himself and
fulfilled his life-work as a statesman. He had laid the foundations of the Irish Republic and proved that his greatness in

triumph was as constant as his stoicism in adversity, poverty and obscurity. His economics, based on List, Berkeley and Swift, were the right ones for his time and problems, and their ultimate result was not inconsistent with his teaching from the beginning. Indeed, ironically enough, as we have seen, it was his nominal rivals who completed his work. Even more ironically, Griffith's programme had been aptly summarized in—of all places—the Karl Marx and Engels proposals for the solution of the Irish Problem in 1867. Though Marx had never heard of the Fintan Lalor formula, he repeated it. The political objective for Ireland must be National Independence if, as is probable, dual monarchy or federation proves impossible. Economically, Irish *industrial* independence must of necessity be based on a system of protection and tariffs until Irish industry is strong enough to face free trade and foreign competition. Marx and Griffith alike, had taken this from Frederick List. Marx added that the Irish Landlord System must be overthrown completely, as it was the basis of the British régime. Events, of course, worked out very differently from the expectations of both men. Yet in the sequel, the prophets were justified. In fact, through the years of transition, Griffith's basic ideas worked out to their logical conclusion. Griffith's economic protective system was rigidly enforced by the first Free State Government. Forty years later, List's formula that Protection inevitably ends in the establishment of free markets, relaxed tariffs, in short, of Free Trade was amply demonstrated. As we have seen, the Irish Land problem was solved in large part pacifically. Politically, too, Griffith's prophecy of 1922 was fulfilled: 'The Treaty Settlement is no more a final settlement than we are the final generation.' Griffith's successors, and his colleagues of the time, lived to proclaim an Irish Republic. Griffith's opponents of 1922 lived on to complete his economic programme with the famous slogan of Mr Lemass: 'The economic foundation of Irish freedom is the task of this generation.'

Paradoxically, Sinn Féin's gravest political defeat came on the issue of Partition which culminated in the Ulster Boundary Commission and Agreement of 1925. Collins and Griffith,

three years before, had signed the 1922 Articles of Agreement
because all too guilelessly they had accepted Lloyd George's
slick and treacherous assurances that the Ulster Clauses of that
Agreement prevented all danger of partition. The deadlock on
the Ulster Clauses was forced open in 1925 by the compromise
reached between representatives of the British Government, the
Free State Government and the Government of Northern
Ireland. It is true an important sop was thrown to the Free
State by the complete cancellation of any liability for a share
in the British National debt. This barely saved the faces of the
Free State representatives. Yet in Ireland, the price was deemed
too high, and appalled all sections of Irish opinion from the
most moderate to the most extreme. It struck at the axiomatic
national loathing of partition now legalized in a formal document by Irish representatives for the first time in history.

Sinn Féin, in fact, won over the surviving Liberals and
descendants of the United Irishmen. Nowhere was Sinn Féin
more fervently accepted than in these Ulster circles traditionally
attached to the ideals of the French Revolution, of civil and
religious liberty. They were the very authors in the past of the
Irish Republic itself. From the beginning, Sinn Féin had waged
a ruthless war on the Catholic sectarianism of the Ancient
Order of Hibernians; and moreover, had made its converts in
the ranks of the left-wing of Ulster Unionism, the break-away
Independent Orange Order. The relations between the Ulster
Volunteers and the Irish Volunteers in the North were cordial,
and even co-operative. At the Larne gun-running, April 23,
1914, a prominent Irish Republican Leader lent his car to land
the Ulster rifles. In the same month a Sinn Féin Convention
in Dublin made a determined effort to reach agreement with
Ulster. The Convention offered increased representation in any
future Irish Parliament on the basis of population, rateable
value and bulk of trade. These proposals won the approval of
the Belfast Trades Council, but were ignored completely by the
Tory and Unionist political leaders.

It is significant that Sinn Féin during the years with which I
am dealing, 1916 to 1926, appeared to us at the time to have
begun with defeat and ended with defeat. In 1917, those who

believed in Sinn Féin were an insignificant and persecuted minority, or in Redmond's words 'small enough to be crushed in the hollow of my hand'. Equally contemptuous and hostile were all the dominant and influential elements of Irish life—the wealthy classes, the large farmers, the Church, the Press. Yet, this insignificant minority was possessed by a fanatical conviction of its inevitable triumph. Whatever the forces against it, on its side were the intellectual and national forces for which Griffith had provided a platform, an inspiration, and a focus in his *United Irishmen* for nearly twenty years.

In 1917 he was a chastened prophet, justified in ways he had not dreamed of. Ireland had heard his message at last, and he was beginning to speak for a minority no more. Moreover, events had filled a role which Griffith had consistently refused to fill; for the first time since the deaths of O'Connell and Parnell, a national leader had arisen to dominate political life—in Griffith's own phrase 'as a statesman and soldier'—in Eamon de Valera, soon to be the symbol representing Ireland to the outside world, of Irish resistance and resurgence. The shadows of defeat lifted. The new leader and the surge of popular enthusiasm welded Sinn Féin into an irresistible force that within two years had put it into power in Ireland. Casement's dream was realized; the Irish question was no longer a British internal issue. It had been moved to an international plane.

The 1925 settlement gave President Cosgrave a nominal victory. It was to prove the prelude to his eventual exit from office in 1932 after his long and most fruitful lease of power. Yet, with the exception of Ulster, he had carried Griffith's programme as far as was then possible. Michael Collin's closest friend, Batt O'Connor, gave the Free State judgement on the Boundary crisis, when he protested in a controversy with Mr. Robert Barton eight years later that Mr. Cosgrave was in 1925 taunted with his inability to fight a second Civil War over Clause 12 of the Treaty against the solid united forces of the British Government and the Orangemen. The truth was, it was Sinn Féin's darkest hour, and the dawn of its victory remote indeed.

Yet as history tells us, within ten years Cosgrave's opponents had carried out to the fullest possible extent Griffith's programme, as the time became ripe.

History followed its inevitable, confusing, contradictory course. As Hegel's law has it: history is a progress through antagonisms to harmony, from thesis to antithesis, and eventually to synthesis. There was indeed something in it, in spite of George Orwell's jibe that these are but three weird sisters invented by the Germans to distract earnest students. Sinn Féin, indeed passed through, in its years of transition, every phase of that historical process, from the thesis of republicanism, to the antithesis of dual monarchy, to the harmonizing synthesis of 'external association'.

4

THE SOCIAL REVOLUTION
THAT NEVER WAS

By Patrick Lynch

WHY DID THE RISING of 1916 fail to produce also a social revolution of corresponding significance and consequence? What happened to avert it? Was it betrayed? Such questions ignore many circumstances. They disregard, for instance, the fact that by 1916 most agricultural holdings had been purchased by their occupiers, subject to land annuities, which were not then a matter of contention. The tenant had become a proprietor, the owner of his land; and little land remained, to which the system of voluntary purchase could be applied. Moreover, rural Ireland had profited from the introduction of the Old Age Pension. In addition, high prices during the Great War were bringing unprecedented prosperity to Irish agriculture, from which, of course, the bigger farmers benefited most. In rural Ireland thoughts of social revolution were held only by a minority—the articulate few and by those who had no stake in war prosperity.

Middle class leadership in Ireland had been firmly established by Daniel O'Connell. His triumph was to merge the peasants and the middle class and to set them both on the road towards political and social progress. His towering eminence over-shadowed the nineteenth century in Ireland and survived even the reassessments of his own immediate achievements. He had unified his people around a single issue, Catholic Emancipation, and they retained this unity and solidarity even when they

forgot its originator. From O'Connell onwards, the middle
class provided, for the most part, political leadership, a leadership that, naturally, tended to be conservative. As a result,
every new movement in the national field after O'Connell
was to the left of the middle class.

The Fenian Movement, predominantly an urban movement,
was made up of people who had migrated from the land or
whose fathers had been dispossessed of it. Once established, the
Fenian tradition continued from 1860 right until 1922 to act
as a spearhead of national advance. The Fenians organized all
discontented elements against British rule and continued to do
so until a specifically labour movement emerged to come into
conflict with the Fenian claim to national leadership. This
labour movement was to reach its zenith under James Connolly,
whose policies combined political nationalism with the strongest
possible advocacy of working class aims and purposes.

From the time of the Land League onwards the lower middle
classes in the towns constituted the revolutionary wing of Irish
politics. The Fenians on the left urged the middle class into a
more progressive policy. According as Home Rule became
weak, the heirs to the Fenian tradition pressed for more
extreme action. Sinn Féin, deriving directly from the Fenian
inspiration, led to the end of British rule in Ireland. The Fenian
and Sinn Féin movements alike were composed mainly of the
poor and the sons and daughters of the dispossessed and the
disinherited. National aims rather than social aims were their
inspiration. The Irish working classes, less socially alert than
their counterparts in other countries, were more distinguished
for militant nationalism than for social radicalism. The middle
and working classes combined to advance the national idea of
independence. Colonialism had to be destroyed before internal
rifts and class conflicts could become clarified.

Constitutionalism failed as a solution to Irish politics after
the Ulster gun-running at Larne. The failure was confirmed
after the Curragh Mutiny. Here lay the immediate origins of
the 1916 rising. Henceforward, people saw that British Governments could be intimidated by pressure groups in Ireland; by
Carson in Ulster and cavalry officers in the Curragh. The Larne

gun-running and the Curragh Mutiny, as successful attempts to defy constitutional government, marked Ireland's contribution to the beginning of European Fascism. And so it was that James Connolly, whose natural opponents might seem to have been the Dublin business men who had fought James Larkin in 1913, found himself fighting the cause not of a class but of a people. Primarily he was fighting the battle of a dependent colonial people against imperialism but, as he said of Fintan Lalor, as might, indeed, be said of himself, he 'advocated his principles as part of the creed of the democracy of the world, and not merely as applicable only to the incidents of the struggle of Ireland against England'. For Connolly, the first Great War was a struggle between one group of capitalists and another.

The Irish Parliamentary Party ceased to carry its traditional influence once it supported Ireland's participation in the Great War, and with Home Rule in abeyance, the fortunes of the Party began to decline. Sinn Féin had ceased to become an active force with the formation of the Irish Volunteers in 1913. John Redmond's recruiting speeches gathered support for the Irish Volunteers, who were in favour of neutrality. The aim of the Volunteers was England's difficulty being Ireland's opportunity. The Citizen Army under Connolly was, of course, also neutral. In other European countries socialist parties had found themselves reluctantly supporting the war. In Ireland, however, the situation was quite different; and national and socialist interests, instead of being in conflict, were co-operating. They were both opposed to the war, at whatever cost. Connolly regarded the war as an imperialist one from the outset and hence justified his position as a socialist in opposition to it.

The struggle against conscription more than anything else revealed the gulf between the official Irish Party and the Irish masses, even though fighting in France were many Irishmen whose love of Ireland was probably no less intense than that of those who remained at home. The Irish Party opposed conscription for Ireland because it knew the spirit of Ireland was against conscription. Connolly had opposed the war on principle.

Ever since 1902 there had been moves towards the foundation

of a separate Irish Labour Party, mainly through the efforts
of the Irish Trade Union Congress, but little effective support
was organized until the rise of 'Larkinism', which became a
new and dynamic form of labour activity after the tremendous
struggle against very unequal odds in the 1913 lock-out. There
were, however, conflicting views about a Labour Party. Some
Trades Unionists found the Irish Parliamentary Party an
adequate mouthpiece. Others maintained that as there were
political unionists as well as nationalists in Ireland, a separate
Labour Party was necessary. By 1911, labour supporters were
already drifting from the Irish Parliamentary Party. The very
possibility of Home Rule persuaded the Irish Trades Union
Congress that the time was ripe for a separate Irish Labour
Party, and in 1912, Congress gave instructions for the drafting
of a constitution. Labour feared that some aspects of the
proposed Home Rule Bill might be dangerous as it might give
less representation to the larger towns than to the rural areas—
a crucial admission that labour strength lay in the towns.
Meanwhile, Congress complained that neither the British
Labour Party nor the Irish Party would take the initiative in
meeting the grievances of Irish labour. And so, under pressure
from Connolly, Thomas Johnson and James Larkin, a separate
Irish Labour Party was formed to secure Irish labour representation in Parliament and all public bodies and to co-operate
with workers in other countries for the common advancement
of labour. Before any election took place, however, the Great
War had begun, and Larkin had left for the U.S.A. leaving
Connolly a dominant figure in the Irish labour movement,
which was based on the Irish Trades Union Congress and
associated with the Citizen Army. An organized social revolutionary movement existed at last, though its activities were
largely restricted to Dublin and other urban areas. Its fearless
attitude towards the war was expressed in challenging words
inscribed on the façade of Liberty Hall: 'We serve neither King
nor Kaiser'. Vigorously opposing the recruiting campaigns for
the British Army in sustained eloquence, brilliant journalism
and active organization, Connolly was led to summarize the
programme of labour in the *Workers' Republic* in January 1916

by declaring 'that the time for Ireland's Battle is Now, the place for Ireland's Battle is Here'; and so the green flag of Ireland was hoisted over Liberty Hall early in April. The political and social aims of the coming rising had been fused. Connolly, however, made little impression on rural areas, but there were exceptions.

The rising of 1916 had killed the socially militant Connolly and other leaders. The way was now open for the original supporters of Sinn Féin to take the leadership. With Griffith dominating the national movement, the social aims of the revolution, as Connolly conceived them, were put aside; opposition to England and national solidarity became the only issue. Griffith emerged as the undisputed leader of the Sinn Féin Party. After the eclipse of the Irish Party in 1918, internal politics in Ireland were concerned mainly with the co-operation and conflict between two forces. One of these forces, Sinn Féin, mainly the middle and lower middle classes of the towns; the other, class conscious workers' organizers in the labour movement. On both sides the decisive influence of urban elements was large and obvious. Gradually the middle classes generally moved towards Sinn Féin and this naturally tended to introduce into Sinn Féin an element of conservatism. The future of Ireland was now largely in the hands of Sinn Féin. And Sinn Féin was determined not to confuse the political struggle by becoming involved directly in any clash of social interests that might divide the growing numbers of mixed supporters it had gathered to itself. Their task was made easier by labour's decision not to participate directly in the dramatic deliberations of the first Dáil.

The social aspirations of the first Irish Republic were incorporated in the Democratic Programme adopted at its first sitting by Dáil Éireann on January 21, 1919. The document forming the basis of the programme was drafted by the late Thomas Johnson and subsequently redrafted with important changes by our former President, Mr. Seán T. Ó Ceallaigh. Mr. Ó Ceallaigh has paid tribute to his collaborators, mainly Thomas Johnson and William O'Brien.

Close contact at the time was being maintained between

Sinn Féin and the Irish Volunteers on the one hand and labour
on the other through Johnson, O'Brien and Cathal O'Shannon.
All three were involved in the common national struggle. They
were also among the delegates appointed by the Irish Labour
Party and the Trade Union Congress to the first post World
War International Socialist and Labour Conference at Berne.
Thus, in the drafting of the programme, the Dáil was in close
contact with labour in deciding what the social programme of
Dáil Éireann should be.

According to Mr. Cathal O'Shannon who is the only
authorative source on the subject, Mr. Seán T. Ó Ceallaigh
contributed about one-third of the programme as adopted by
the Dáil. Johnson, who, of course, was not a member, contributed two-thirds, and about half of his draft was omitted.

It would be quite wrong to assume that the modified draft
produced by Mr. Ó Ceallaigh eliminated all the socialist
content of the original. There were omissions, it is true. The
draft no longer declared that 'no private right to property is good
against the public right of the nation'—words ironically taken
from Patrick Pearse writing in the *Sovereign People* of March 31,
1916. Pearse was already being expurgated. Nor did the final draft
declare that the 'nation must ever retain the right to resume possession of such soil or wealth whenever the trust is abused or the
trustee fails to give faithful service'. This, however, was Johnson
rather than Pearse, not, at least, Pearse's actual words.

The programme, as eloquently moved in Irish in the Dáil by
General Richard Mulcahy stated 'It shall be the first duty of
the Government of the Republic to make provision for the
physical, mental and spiritual well-being of the children, to
ensure that no child shall suffer hunger or cold from lack of
food, clothing or shelter, that all shall be provided with the
means and facilities requisite for their proper education and
training as citizens of a free and Gaelic Ireland'. For some
inexplicable reason a sentence was dropped from the Johnson
draft providing with innocuous vagueness that: 'A condition
precedent to such education is to encourage by every reasonable
means the most capable and sympathetic men and women to
devote their talents to the education of the young'.

Even though the Johnson draft was reduced, of much of its socialist content, provision was made for public enterprise. All aspirations influenced by the Soviet experiment or by Syndicalist ideas were, however, rejected. From the Johnson draft the following clause was dropped: 'It shall be the purpose of the Government to encourage the organization of the people into Trade Unions and co-operative societies, with a view to the control and administration of the industries by the workers engaged in the industries'. And the final version omitted the next sentence of the original draft which read that 'Wherever the land, the mineral deposits and other forms of productive wealth are wrongfully used or withheld from use to the detriment of the Republic, there the nation shall resume possession without compensation'.

In spite of the changes made in Johnson's document, the redraft by Mr. Seán T. Ó Ceallaigh and proposed for adoption by Dáil Éireann by General Mulcahy remained a radical affirmation of social democratic aspirations. Well, indeed, might Mr. Piaras Beaslai wonder whether the Democratic Programme, read to the Dáil first in Irish by him and in English by Alderman Tom Kelly, would have been supported by the majority of members without amendment if there had been any immediate prospect of putting it into force. Beaslai was probably writing in extreme terms when, discounting the excited atmosphere of the great events in which he took a leading part, he suggests that 'if any charge of insincerity could be made against the first Dáil it would be on this score', that is, on the score of the Democratic programme. Yet the fact remains that this was the solemn social declaration of the first Dáil in 1919, even if afterwards some participants might regard it as a genuflection to the aspirations of the working class interest, whose support was then sorely needed. What is certain, however, is that its emotive content derived from Pearse's work *The Sovereign People*, which, of course, is the source of the statement that the 'Nation's soil and its resources, all wealth and all the wealth-producing processes of the Nation, and . . . all right to private property must be subordinated to the public right and welfare'.

It is hard to disagree, however, with the late P. S. O'Hegarty
that all this was accepted, rather uncritically, as it was wrapped
up in the language and presented as the legacy of Pearse. As
the whole session of the Dáil lasted less than two hours the time
given to the Democratic programme can hardly have been
more than half an hour. The declaration was neither critically
considered nor systematically examined. The resolutions were
proposed, seconded and adopted unanimously. Their context
certainly derived from an Irish social democratic tradition, but
it would seem to be far removed from the spirit of the Dáil,
whose main purpose was a re-affirmation of Irish political
independence. As O'Hegarty has said, it was a great and
historic occasion, and the significance of it ruled out everything
save emotion. If Mr. de Valera, Arthur Griffith, Michael
Collins or Mr. Ernest Blythe, had been present, more moderate
or at least other views might have been expressed. In the
absence of decisive and resolute leadership the heady atmosphere of excitement triumphed.

It is clear from General Mulcahy's speech that he, at least,
was fully aware of the social implications of the programme but,
with few exceptions, the members of the first Dáil were primarily
concerned with achieving the national independence of a
formerly dependent colony. They were instinctively determined
on national independence and even largely unaware of social
conflicts that might well be as acute in the free Ireland of their
aspirations as in the colonial dependency from which they
wanted to escape. Connolly was dead and no leader remained,
who was sufficiently versed in the social democratic tradition
and sufficiently articulate, to explain the real significance of the
Democratic Programme. Moreover, religious influences must be
taken into account. In spite of the conservatism of the Catholic
hierarchy, there had always been a politically radical element,
however small, among the clergy, but even that element was
usually cautious on social issues; and the laity was fully aware
of the fact. The Labour Party had exerted an influence, but
they were prompters in the wings rather than actors on the
stage.

The Irish Labour Party had contested neither the elections

of 1918 nor of 1921 in the belief that by abstaining they were leaving the people free to express themselves unambiguously on the political issue of self-determination for nationhood. Labour would not be a party to vote-splitting on the vital issue. Yet, without extracting any concessions from Sinn Féin, they committed themselves to an arid and ambiguous neutrality. Whether consciously or not they were influenced by the doctrines of Arthur Griffith who vigorously, and often vehemently, sought to keep Sinn Féin aloof from the social conflict. Wherever Griffith saw socialist influence he sensed British influence. 'The man', he wrote, 'who injures Ireland whether he does it in the name of Imperialism or of Socialism is Ireland's enemy'. The country should not be divided into hostile camps on any account. Not all members of Sinn Féin agreed with him. But his doctrine prevailed, and so the Labour Party did not press what was now regarded as their sectional interest against the national interest. There was no one of Connolly's stature to match the persuasive arguments of Griffith. One can imagine how differently Connolly might have interpreted that historical situation.

Sporadically, advantage was taken of the unsettled conditions in the country to show that an aggressive spirit of social unrest still existed. In May 1920 the workers in Cleeves' factory in Knocklong, county Limerick, settled a strike by declaring a soviet. Their example was followed by the miners in Arigna, county Leitrim. In Bruree, county Limerick, the workers' soviet mills, as they described themselves, announced: 'We make bread, not profits.' But the Trades Union Congress looked on these experiments with a lack of enthusiasm. It adopted generalized resolutions about labour's role; and resolutions do not make a social revolution.

After the Treaty, the Griffith doctrine of Sinn Féin continued to find expression in the attitude and behaviour of the Labour Party. Labour officially deplored the split in the nationalist ranks. The newspaper *The Voice of Labour* even pointed out that 'the Dáil and not labour had been entrusted by the Irish people with authority and responsibility'. The Labour Party embarked on a policy of apparent neutrality which was to shape its character if not its tactics for more than a generation. It sought to achieve unity between those who were now supporting the Treaty and those who were opposing it. Yet against the Treaty there were people such as Liam Mellows, who wrote 'that the commercial interests and the merchants are on the side of the Treaty. We are back to Tone—and it is just as well—relying on the men of no property. The stake in the country people were never with the Republic; they will always be against it until it wins'.

Neither Treaty nor anti-Treaty parties officially favoured a class struggle. In February 1922 the Labour Party decided by a large majority to contest the forthcoming elections. In addition, a motion in favour of a plebiscite on the Treaty before the general election was carried by a large majority, but the resolution, although pressed by Thomas Johnson, made no impression on Griffith, who insisted that the election should decide the Treaty issue. The incipient threat of civil war impelled the Labour Party towards achieving a peaceful solution even to the extent of calling a one-day strike in favour of peace.

Eighteen labour candidates, where they seemed to have a reasonable chance of success, were put forward in the election, mainly members of the Transport Union. The Labour Party overtly avoided taking sides on the Treaty issue, but its very intervention in the election could be constructed as support for the Treaty. It is true that this intervention had not been expected by Collins or by Mr. de Valera, whose idea was a coalition drawn from a single list of candidates on both sides in proportion to their strength in the existing Dáil. It was added, however, that 'every and any interest' was free to contest the election. Seventeen of the labour candidates were elected. Those elected had put forward Trade Union viewpoints. Thus, the election threw no light on social issues nor did any candidate advocate social revolution. It would be hard, indeed, to read any desire for social revolution into the results. Labour was satisfied with its election achievements, and in the prevailing mood was not prepared to seek more radical objectives. It had taken a long time to build up a labour organization and Thomas Johnson was taking no risks. The Transport Union, the chief supporter of the Labour Party, showed at its twenty-eighth Annual Meeting in August 1922 that it gave full support to this policy. In 1923 James Larkin returned from the U.S.A. He sought immediately to become General Secretary; if he had joined as an ordinary member he might have dominated the union in six months. On May 14 he quoted the guiding principle of what he wrongly attributed to the Jesuits 'In things essential, unity; in things doubtful, liberty, but in all things, charity'. Unfortunately, this advice was not followed and so a unified campaign for social revolution never took place. Instead there was a divided labour movement, largely on personalities and with internal divisions, the Labour Party faced the election of 1923. The party contested twenty-six out of twenty-nine constituencies and put forward forty-three candidates, only fourteen of whom were returned. Strife had split the labour movement.

Political liberation of the Irish Free State had been secured. The social conflict, as seen from Wolfe Tone to Connolly, and indeed by socialist republicans after him, had become submerged. Labour had officially stood on the sideline from 1919 to 1921. By 1923 its leaders had less radical aspirations. Thomas Johnson, leader of the party, was deploring the moral as well as the economic ruin of the civil war. Labour became a small party of individuals, relying less on a broad general socialist policy for its support, than on personal support for its candidates. The Griffith concept of classless nationhood, that labour must wait, was victorious. The radical working class had no clear leadership or class-consciousness. Yeats saw a terrible beauty born in 1916, but the vision of union between social revolutionaries and political separatists survived only in individual cases. There was now no labour leader sufficiently big in stature to carry through the doctrines and the policies of Connolly. After 1916 labour and nationalism drifted apart and labour took mainly to industrial organization rather than to political action.

Marx, himself had understood Irish conditions well, as indeed had Lenin, perhaps even better, though Lenin was surely being somewhat academic when he declared that 'The misfortune of the Irish is that they rose prematurely, when the European revolt of the proletarist had not yet matured'. Yet, Lenin fully understood Connolly's motives in acting as he did in 1916 instead of waiting for the European socialists who were then compromising themselves and their principles on the issue of the Great War. It is easy, too, for the text-book Marxist to hint at Connolly's syndicalist tendencies and at his failure to create a revolutionary political party to unite and lead workers in town and country. That was impossible in the context of the time. The national issue of independence was the only national rallying point at which all classes could be united. Moreover, the small farmers had traditionally taken their leaders from the middle class and believed that they had been well served by them from O'Connell to Parnell. Many workers and farmers still followed John Redmond right up to 1916. Rural Ireland was greatly indebted to the Irish Party for land reform which had brought benefits to all classes. Lenin might denounce, as he did, in 1913 the land annuities as a tribute paid in respect of former plunder. Whatever socialist republicans might say, the Irish farmers were contented because most of them now owned their land; the bank balances accumulated during the Great War reflected the satisfaction of the bigger farmers and their support for law and order. For them a social revolution had in fact taken place, and the country now sought a revolution of a different type. The workers in the towns, the small farmers and labourers, would have to wait for other days and other leaders. There was no rapid expansion in the numbers of industrial workers in the years immediately after the Treaty. In spite of the enthusiasm of Sinn Féin for protection, industrial development was prudent and cautious; and the power of imposing tariffs was sparingly used. The Fiscal Inquiry Committee of 1923 set down the principles by which the development of native industrialization should be guided, and these principles were generally observed in a policy called 'selective protection'. Thirty years later only one-fifth of the working population was engaged in manufacturing industry, a vastly smaller proportion than in most other European countries. The thinking of the five economists of the Fiscal Inquiry Committee of 1923, with its cold analytical reports, was a far cry from the glowing and heart-warming spontaneity of the Democratic Programme of 1919—and very much further from the social revolution that never was.

In 1920 there were over 102,000 members of the Irish Transport and General Workers Union. After that year, its membership steeply declined until eventually it was reduced by half. The post-war agricultural depression caused such a fall in membership, that the Union ceased to cater for the 40,000 agricultural workers that it had in its ranks in 1920. In 1924, many members, especially in Dublin, seceded to the newly-established Workers Union of Ireland, including the dockers, who were now back again under James Larkin's leadership. The Transport Union decided not to recognize the new union officially and so, members of the Transport Union were free to take jobs from striking members of Larkin's union and yet remain respectable trade unionists—in the eyes, at least of the Transport Union. All the while, of course, many members of the Irish Trades Union Congress remained members of British based unions as they believed that they were paid more in strike pay and benefit than they contributed in union dues. Unity, indeed, was lacking in Irish labour.

There was little use for idealism and less scope for utopianism in the Irish Free State of 1923. The situation was now very different from what it had been in 1919. A native government had to carry the immense responsibilities of administering a country emerging from the confusion, conflict and bitterness of a terrible civil war. Labour, largely because of its own behaviour, presented no serious challenge to the economic or social philosophy of the Government; the role of labour was now sectional or marginal, in no sense crucial or central; it was merely a minority party and a well-disciplined one. In the circumstances, not all members of the Government could be regarded as in sympathy with any practical effort to implement the high aspirations of the Democratic Programme. Their Civil Service advisors, no doubt, gave them little encouragement towards changing social categories that now owed more to the conventional wisdom of Whitehall than to Pearse or Connolly.

The Government, in fact, were acting in accord with Professor Brogan's maxim that the politician's duty is not to meet the specifications laid down by Plato or Hegel; but the endless, varied and unpredictable demands of situations created by varied human wills.

5

THE CONDUCT OF THE ANGLO-IRISH WAR, (JANUARY 1919 TO THE TRUCE IN JULY 1921)

By G. A. Hayes-McCoy

'THE DEFENSIVE', said Karl Marx, 'is the death of every armed rising.' It was the death of 1916. As it occurred— for its original plan was perhaps different—the revolt of Easter Week in that year could have had only one military end. The Irish Volunteers and Irish Citizen Army men committed themselves in Dublin to the defence of fixed positions. In Enniscorthy and county Galway they were dominated by superior forces in positions which they had occupied. In these circumstances they were, like the Paris Communards of 1871 in miniature, bound to succumb in the end to the ruthless application of superior force. In taking up their positions they had limited their ability to manoeuvre; in fact, as events transpired, they had deprived themselves of it altogether. This was a serious handicap in the face of an enemy so much stronger than they were.

They had also committed themselves to acceptance of the full and immediate adverse consequences of defeat. Years later Colonel J. J. O'Connell blamed the Dublin Volunteers for surrendering their arms when they themselves surrendered; but it is difficult to see how they could have saved their weapons for future use. By fighting as they did, P. H. Pearse, the Director of Organization of the Irish Volunteers, and the Volunteers and Citizen Army men whom he led disclosed and committed their whole strength. Their defeat must therefore be a total defeat, by which their armament would be lost and their organizations would suffer. The possibility of this was no doubt in Eoin MacNeill's mind in February, 1916 when he wrote: 'The reproach of the former Irish Volunteers'—he meant the Volunteers of 1782—'is not that they did not fight, but that they did not maintain their organization till their objects had been secured'. MacNeill was Chief-of-Staff of the Volunteers. He did not approve of and did not take part in the rising.

But there were in 1916, as there always are, considerations other than military ones; and, since it was a time of war and Britain was hard pressed in France, the moment had, for some, created its own opportunity, when vigorous action might have extraordinary results. In the event the effect of the harsh suppression of the rising, of the execution of its instigators, and of the ripening of the revolutionary idea among the imprisoned Volunteers and among the public was to convert a military failure into a victory for the separatist movement. Between 1916 and 1918 three by-elections were won by candidates—one of them Eamon de Valera—who had made no pre-election statement of policy and who owed their seats to their being associated in the public mind with abstention from Westminster and adherence to the principles of the rising. At the general election in 1918 the Sinn Féin Party—abstentionists and separatists—won every seat save two for constituencies outside north-east Ulster—seventy-three seats in all—and replaced the Irish Parliamentary Party as representatives of the people. In January 1919 the first Dáil Éireann, or Irish Parliament, met and acclaimed the 1916 proclamation of the Irish Republic.

Ireland, peacefully, constitutionally, and democratically, had declared its preference for a régime which less than three years before a small minority of its citizens had failed to set up in arms.

At this optimistic stage nobody—no group or body which might have brought it about—contemplated another insurrection. Violence had been spoken of in 1918 when conscription was threatened, and the Volunteer Convention of the year before that had empowered its executive to 'declare war' if necessary in resistance of any government attempt to enforce military service; but the First World War was over in 1919, the drums no longer beat for men, and peace was in the air. The hope of Ireland's new leaders—most of them new also to politics—lay not in another appeal to arms but in an appeal to the post-war Peace Conference which, since it was to usher in a new age, might compel Britain to grant self-government to Ireland.

None can have seen—none can have glimpsed—the depths to which Ireland was soon to be plunged. But there were warnings of trouble to come. Irish voters might indulge in heroics, but Britain had responsibilities to discharge. Hers, moreover, was the reality of power and the tradition of coercion. Lord Birkenhead said, speaking at this time of British intentions in Ireland: 'We shall use force and yet more force'. And on January 21, the day on which the Dáil endorsed the declaration of the Republic, the Volunteers used force as well. Two armed policemen were killed at Soloheadbeg, county Tipperary while trying to prevent the seizure of a consignment of gelignite which they had been detailed to guard. This action, although it was not, in fact, the first show of force, has been spoken of as the commencement of what is called in Ireland the Anglo-Irish war, or the Black-and-Tan war, or the Trouble.

One might quote Karl Marx again; after all, his knowledge of revolution, if theoretical, was profound. Marx said—'Never play with insurrection, but when beginning it firmly realize that you must go to the end'. The Irish leaders had not reached the end when those of them who were outside prison met in an Irish parliament in 1919. Their task was not to be as easy as that. The end was to be preceded by violence and bitterness. The shots of Soloheadbeg re-echoed for years.

The Irish Volunteer strength is said to have reached 100,000 in October 1918. The threat of conscription had driven many men into the ranks, however, and the numbers fell off very considerably after the war. Training was rudimentary, and the vast majority was totally unarmed. The Convention of 1917

E

which provided for the reorganization of the Volunteers after the violent interruption of the rising, was the last to meet under British rule. From that time forward until after the truce in 1921 their affairs were controlled, under some measure of Irish Republican Brotherhood influence, by a General Headquarters staff and an executive body in Dublin. The reorganization included an extension of the pre-1916 scheme of territorial companies and battalions and the formation of the whole force into brigades.

When the Dáil set up a government and appointed a Ministry of Defence the Volunteers came under its control. It was claimed that this government, to which they later took an oath of allegiance, was lawfully constituted, and that the Volunteers formed its lawful army in the state of war which was assumed to exist between Ireland and Britain. As the official organ *An tÓglach* put it: 'Every Volunteer is entitled morally and legally, when in the execution of his military duties, to use all legitimate methods of warfare against the soldiers and policemen of the English usurper, and to slay them if it is necessary to do so in order to overcome their resistance.'

Britain ignored this assumption of belligerent rights, however—just as she ignored the claim of the Dáil to govern Ireland. She had over 30,000 troops in Ireland and almost 10,000 armed police, and with this force to back it her government continued to rule the country and continued to treat active Irish hostility as outrage. The fact that, as time went on, Volunteer attacks were developed against the Royal Irish Constabulary, which was discharging the duties of a police force, gave some colour to the consistently reiterated British claim that what she was dealing with in Ireland was not war but civil disturbance.

The position deteriorated. Although Dáil Éireann, in April 1919, contented itself, despite its talk of war, with a resolution that the Constabulary should be 'ostracized socially by the people of Ireland', attacks on policemen grew in frequency. They were motivated primarily by the Volunteer determination to secure arms.

By the winter of 1919–20 hostilities in the south had assumed the aspect of guerrilla war. Neither Dáil Éireann nor Volunteer

Headquarters had given a general direction to this end. In fact these bodies still shared the public dislike of activities which caused casualties on either side. There was no new 'rising'. Nobody laid down the form which hostilities were to take. Circumstances alone—and not for the first time in Irish history—dictated the means by which the great military power of Britain might be met and her claim to rule Ireland might be contested. They were quite different from the means that had been used in 1916.

The Volunteers in 1919 to 1921 did not make the military mistake of fighting on the defensive against a superior power, or of committing their full strength—such as it was—in one place or at one time. They recognized the might of Britain, a victor in the titanic struggle against Germany, and they knew that there were now no 'gallant allies in Europe' (such as the 1916 leaders had claimed) or elsewhere who might support them. They did not attempt another sacrifice of blood; there was a new spirit in the air and men recoiled in disgust from the slaughter of Flanders and Verdun. Besides, they had not the arms for a general rising; no 'Asgard' had come to them, as it had come to the Volunteers in 1914 with the Mauser rifles which had made the Easter Week rising possible. Yet they were a force professing to be military; a voluntary force of the best of Irish youth, determined to serve their country. Theirs was an organization that would be meaningless if, in the face of provocation, and in a world in which old wrongs were everywhere being redressed, it did not try to act its part—a military part. Their leaders were local leaders; their performance ran ahead of the promptings of their Headquarters; in some places they were active, in others not so; always they were practical men who were content to use the means at hand to achieve their purpose. They did not expect a victory overnight, or next week, or next year; and they were idealists too, for they seem never to have contemplated defeat. Circumstances forced them to the extreme of a warfare of their own.

Their methods were impressive. More than 300 years before this when England sought to overrun Ulster Hugh O'Neill's men had perfected a system of fighting which delayed the

English conquest for years. They attacked moving forces of the enemy at places of their own choice. They pressed their attacks home when they saw a chance of success, drew back when they sensed danger, vanished when the enemy counter-attacked. They were difficult to withstand because they sought out and exploited every weakness, difficult to subdue because they held neither towns nor castles and because they suited their tactics to the ground on which they fought. They compelled their antagonists to give up formal warfare and to fight them on their own terms. Above all, until the fatal day of Kinsale, when O'Neill was defeated in a battle in the open field in 1601, they held the tactical initiative and committed themselves only when they knew that success would be certain.

No historian, reading again the story of the Irish struggle of 1919 to 1921, can fail to be impressed by the similarity of method that exists between the performance of the Volunteers and that of these forgotten Ulstermen. We can take it that the Volunteers knew little of O'Neill, and that they certainly had no intention of copying him; but circumstances taught them, as they had taught him, the commonsense of war.

Historically, two strains are discernible in warfare as conducted by the Irish. The first is the war of the countryside, which was adapted to the ground and which suited the limited resources of poor areas. This was the primitive kind. It was most notably exploited by Hugh O'Neill. Colonel Richard Grace used it in 1651 and 1652, the Raparees used it in the war against the Williamites, Joseph Holt and Michael Dwyer used it after the rising of 1798. The second is formal warfare conducted with large and concentrated forces in accordance with changing contemporary practice. The armies of the Catholic Confederation at the middle of the seventeenth century and King James's army at its end practised this kind of war.

Irish insurgents, believing that the proper way to fight was like a 'soldier', that is, in accordance with whatever was the accepted practice of their day, always tried to equip themselves for formal war. Thus the Wexfordmen in 1798 formed line at Vinegar Hill and the Fenian drill of the nineteenth century envisaged close formations of rifles and pikes.

Similarly the Irish Volunteers in 1916 took up battle positions as though they were Belgian regulars and Dublin was Antwerp.

It was an aspiration that died hard. Even Seán Treacy, who fired some of the shots at Soloheadbeg, looked forward in 1918 to warfare of entrenchments and base camps and pike charges.

But Ireland was not unique. Here as elsewhere in the past guerrilla war followed the defeat of regular effort. The Spanish guerrilleros did not take the field until Napoleon had defeated the Spanish armies. The Boers did not begin their two years guerrilla war until Pretoria had fallen. In 1919 when the Irish Volunteers, where their local leadership was aggressive, grew active once more it was to the war of the countryside that, as though by instinct, they turned. They did so because Headquarters had set them no task and it was they who had to lay out the work, but they did so too because 1916 was their regular war and 1916 was over. They were beginning again in another way. As Michael Collins said: 'We organized our army and met the armed patrols and military expeditions which were sent against us in the only way possible. We met them by an organized and bold guerrilla warfare'.

The greatest Volunteer deficiency was in arms and ammunition. Consequently they sought first, as the Fenians had done in 1867, the weapons of the police. Policemen were attacked and disarmed in Cork in March and in July 1918. In April 1919 arms were seized at Araglin police barrack, and in July and August police posts in county Clare were raided. Carrigtwohill barrack, county Cork was the first to be taken after a fight.

But the police were more than purveyors of arms. They were, said de Valera, speaking in the Dáil in 1919, 'no ordinary civil force, as police are in other countries', but 'a military body, armed with rifle and bayonet and revolver as well as baton'. Their history was, he said, 'a continuity of brutal treason against their own people'. No doubt he remembered that they had put down the Fenian rising (and earned their title of Royal for it), just as the Irish Militia had in their time done more than any other component of the British forces to put down the rising of 1798, and as Irish troops serving in the British Army had taken the foremost part in the fighting against the insurgents in

Dublin in 1916. The Constabulary men were the eyes and ears of the administration, the infinitely more efficient successors of the late eighteenth and early nineteenth century Yeomanry Corps, the protectors of what was left of the ascendancy, and the upholders of the established condition of things.

They were also, like the Volunteers, Irishmen. Men of unquestioned courage, superb physique and acknowledged efficiency, the Constabulary, in this twilight of their existence, were caught in a cruel dilemma. They had the loyalty of their service to uphold, but their country was turning against them—not just the extremists and the firebrands, but the whole country. Caught thus and abandoned thus, most of them sought the way of honour, either by resigning or by continuing to do their duty, as they saw it; some became embittered; others grew vengeful and violent and reckless and justified by their nefarious actions the worst accusations that had been levelled against their force.

At first the Volunteers had been content merely to capture the police arms. Gradually their purpose of revolt hardened and they attempted to break the hold which the Constabulary had on the country. They began to burn the barracks. The method which they used in these attacks was the Fenian method. The Fenians had captured Ballyknockane barrack in county Cork and Stepaside and Glencullen barracks in county Dublin in 1867 by firing into them, breaking the windows, and—in one instance—breaking through the roof. They had burnt Bally-knockane. At Glencullen they had sent out pickets to guard against interruption by police reinforcements.

History now repeated itself. During 1920 barracks were attacked in increasing numbers, particularly in Limerick, Clare, Tipperary and Cork. Kilmallock barrack, where twenty-four men had withstood the Fenians, was, in May 1920, defended by twenty-eight. It was attacked by thirty Volunteers, while forty more guarded the approaches. The roof was broken and paraffin pumped in. A bomb started a blaze and the barrack was destroyed, but the garrison, suffering six casualties, held a detached building and kept off the attackers with rifle, rifle grenade and revolver fire. The attack on Hollyford barrack, county Tipperary was similar. Drangan surrendered with the loss of the police weapons. Rear Cross was burnt after a five hour fight. Everywhere the pattern was the same—a close and carefully planned attack, a stubborn resistance, and—more often than not—the destruction of the post.

In the face of such attacks police authority in several areas was seriously weakened. Hundreds of smaller barracks were abandoned and their constables concentrated in the larger ones. At Easter 1920 over 300 of these abandoned buildings were burnt or otherwise destroyed by the Volunteers. The police admitted that the withdrawal from the outlying areas meant 'the handing over of tracts of country to the enemy', but they had no alternative. They were, they said, 'losing men every day from retirements and resignations, and getting practically no recruits'. In June 1920 the police at Listowel mutinied. In August it was officially admitted that there had been 556 resignations from the Constabulary in the previous two months. Despite efforts to make it more militaristic, the force was beginning to crack.

Troops, of whom the country was full—troops in battle order with all the paraphernalia of Flanders, from tanks to entrenching tools—were of course employed to the utmost in conjunction with the police in an effort to maintain the traditional law and order. They also were targets for the Volunteers. Although ordinarily military barracks were too strong to be attacked, Mallow cavalry barrack was taken by a ruse and two machine guns and twenty-seven rifles captured, and there were many other brushes with the troops. After the appointment of Sir Hamar Greenwood as Chief Secretary and Sir Nevil Macready as General Officer Commanding British Forces in March and April 1920, and with the intention of 'stamping out rebellion with a strong hand', reinforcements of over 7,000 men were brought in, together with great quantities of warlike supplies. There were in 1921 more than 35,000 troops in Ireland. But, in keeping with the British claim that the Irish hostilities were not war, it was most notably the police, rather than the military, who were reinforced. This was done, failing further Irish material, by drawing on Britain. In March 1920 the first of the

British recruits for the Constabulary arrived. These were the notorious Black-and-Tans—violent, undisciplined and poor fighters. They were joined in July by the first 500 men of a new formation, later to reach more than double that strength, the Auxiliary Division of the Royal Irish Constabulary. It was these special forces, introduced to make Ireland 'an appropriate hell for those whose trade is agitation and whose method is murder', who gave the later stages of the struggle their peculiar character of ruthlessness and terror, and who did so much to alienate the remaining support for Britain in Ireland. Against them were employed the developed tactics of the Volunteers.

These were the tactics of the ambush. In Ireland the use of guns to ambush one's foes is a practice at least as old as 1538, when Lord Leonard Grey, the viceroy, made use of it. As the winter of 1920 drew in and the concentration, the increasing militarization and the extraordinary reinforcement of the police limited the possibility of further attacks on the barracks, the Volunteers found in the ambush the answer to a problem of tactics and a problem of supply. The ambushing of lorry-borne forces of the crown, which now replaced as warfare the traditional rising, permitted the capture of arms and ammunition, without which the struggle could not be continued, and it provided a means of attacking by a series of limited actions a vastly superior force. It allowed for the use of small, trained groups of Volunteers, who became more efficient as time went on, and who gained experience as much from their unsuccessful as from their successful actions. It was perfectly adapted to the Volunteer system of organization. The local companies, operating underground, were everywhere ready to support the fighting columns, which appeared in the open to strike at their foes only when they chose to do so, and then vanished again among the people.

The Volunteers, up to the time of the Truce, can never have had many more than a thousand rifles, practically all of which—with their ammunition—had been captured from their opponents. They supplemented these weapons with shotguns, revolvers and, at the end, a few machine guns, and with grenades and land mines which they made themselves. Their fighting units or flying columns were each an independent force of thirty or forty men, sometimes less. Organized first in Dublin, Headquarters ordered all brigades to form such active service units at the end of 1920.

From the ambushes of Toureen and Kilmichael in Cork and Granard and Ballinalee in Longford in November 1920 the roll mounted. At Crossbarry in March 1921, where the ambush technique was perhaps seen at its best, Commandant Tom Barry's West Cork Brigade flying column, 104 strong, successfully attacked a strong lorry-borne force of troops and then fought its way through encircling forces more than three times its own number, an operation worthy of De Wet.

With such limited resources, and with these tactics—which were in miniature the tactics of the Yellow Ford brought up to date—this extraordinary war went on, a war waged in the midst of a country trying to carry on its everyday business as usual.

The British, who in 1920 still feared the outbreak of a general rising, found that advances in the technique of war actually favoured their opponents. In the country ambushes rifles were better in attack than in defence. In the Dublin streets, to which ambushes were soon extended, the Volunteers found that pistols and revolvers suited their purpose better than rifles, and the Dublin rifles were soon collected and sent into the country to equip the columns there. In the city streets too, hand grenades were, for the Volunteers, effective and procurable weapons. Motor transport, an element still new in war, invited ambush and delivered the crown forces piecemeal into the hands of the Volunteers. Tied to the roads, the troops and police could be immobilized by obstructions and bridge breaking.

Irish determination, under the inspired leadership of Michael Collins and encouraged by success, hardened as the months went by. The country was behind the Volunteers. It was symptomatic of the change in public opinion that had taken place since 1916 that local authorities now showed sympathy with those who struggled against Britain and that the railway men in some places supported the Volunteers by refusing to transport British warlike supplies. It was too a vital ingredient of such success as the Irish achieved that hostilities were not confined to one area, or to a few places, and that the cities, and particularly Dublin, were involved as well as the countryside. The Dublin units of the Volunteers, at least one of which could, before its rifles were sent into the country, have paraded as well equipped with captured Lee Enfields and bayonets as a regular British formation, did much to provide weapons and ammunition for their comrades elsewhere. It was something new in Irish history that movements of British forces were contested in the Dublin streets, and the large scale operation of the attack by the Dublin Brigade of the Volunteers on the Custom House in May 1921 showed the British authorities how ruthless their opponents could be. On the other hand, Britain, exasperated by an assault that she considered underhand merely because it was unorthodox, felt herself increasingly forced to extremes.

Britain was not, and could not have been, militarily defeated. There was an answer to the methods of the Volunteers—for the country ambush the armoured car and machine gun, for the attack in the city streets the foot patrol. The concentration camps might have been enlarged. It should not have been impossible to deny the Volunteers ammunition. The limit of terror had not been reached. But the price of victory on those terms, in the twentieth century and between two civilized and not unfriendly peoples, would have been too great. Terror was unworthy of Britain. It was to her credit that—even though belatedly—she recognized that it was. It was the British who called for the truce.

6

DÁIL ÉIREANN AND THE ARMY: UNITY AND DIVISION

(1919–1921)

By Kevin B. Nowlan

O N JANUARY 21, 1919, Dáil Éireann met for the first time and solemnly adopted a declaration of independence ratifying the establishment of the republic which had been proclaimed in Dublin on Easter Monday 1916. The Dáil's declaration contained one very significant passage. The republic, it stated, had been proclaimed in 1916 by 'the Irish Republican Army acting on behalf of the Irish people'. Behind that apparently simple formula lay a complex constitutional situation which owed much to the unusual circumstances and difficulties under which the first Dáil had come into being.

The Dáil was by no means the senior among the radical nationalist bodies in existence in 1919. It was in fact the youngest. The Irish Volunteers were older, and most venerable of all was the Irish Republican Brotherhood which could trace its history back to the 1850s and, in a sense, indirectly back to 1848–9 when some among the Young Irelanders turned to more secret forms of revolutionary activity following the failure of the rising of 1848. Put another way, it could be said that the armed forces of the republic had existed before the republic had actual parliamentary institutions. But the position was even more complicated than that. There were some who argued that an Irish republic existed before the declaration made in 1916. The constitution of the secret, oath-bound Irish Republican Brotherhood stated that the 'Supreme Council of the Irish Republican Brotherhood is hereby declared in fact as well as right the sole government of the Irish Republic until Ireland secures absolute national independence and a permanent republican government is established'. For the I.R.B. the republic had been 'virtually established', to use their own phrase, with the formation of a provisional government in February 1867, just before the abortive rising of March in the same year. The constitution of the I.R.B., as revised in 1920, again proclaimed, despite the establishment of Dáil Éireann, that the Supreme Council was 'the sole government of the Irish Republic'. There is evidence which suggests that the constitution was amended on this critical point before the end of 1919, but that amendment was not incorporated in the text of the constitution as issed in 1920. One wonders why.

The I.R.B., despite many vicissitudes, provided an element of continuity in the history of Irish republicanism. The same cannot be said of Sinn Féin, the parent of Dáil Éireann, or indeed of the Irish Volunteers, at least in their origins. The events of 1916 presented Sinn Féiners with a challenge. They could either cling to Griffith's notion of a dual monarchy or they could come to terms with republicanism. In 1917, a year of uncertainty and transition in the history of Irish Nationalism, the Sinn Féin movement and its leaders finally accepted a compromise formula at the October convention. Article two of the new Sinn Féin constitution declared that the aim of the movement was to secure 'international recognition of Ireland as an independent Irish republic' and, having achieved that international recognition, the Irish people could then 'by referendum freely choose their own form of government'. The way back to a dual monarchy or any other political settlement with Great Britain was in this way left open. But, in effect, the reorganized Sinn Féin movement had accepted republicanism though, in the light of subsequent developments, the reservations on the ultimate character of the Irish constitution must not be forgotten. The election, in October 1917, of Eamon de Valera to the presidency of Sinn Féin: and then to the presidency of the Volunteers strengthened the swing in Sinn Féin towards republicanism and away from Griffith's earlier preference for a monarchical order in Ireland.

The executions and arrests which followed the 1916 rising had done much to disrupt the Irish Volunteers. The reorganization of the force at the end of 1917 was the first serious attempt to make good the damage that had been done. The Volunteers had not been founded as a specifically republican movement. Their original constitution had defined their aim as being 'to secure and maintain the rights and liberties common to all the people of Ireland'. The I.R.B. had recognized the value of the Volunteers as a 'front organization' and the split between the pro- and anti-Redmondites as well as the rising of 1916 itself had ensured that by 1917, the surviving Irish Volunteers were essentially republican in outlook. Their newspaper *An tÓglach* was able to say, in August 1918, 'the Irish Volunteers are a military body pure and simple. They are the army of the Irish Republic, the agents of the national will.' These 'agents of the national will' had, however, their own independent organization, independent of Sinn Féin and of Dáil Éireann too. The Volunteer movement had its central executive, and its constitution could only be amended by a convention made up of delegates drawn from all the units. In structure, therefore, it resembled more a civilian society than a military body; not surprisingly in view of the circumstances under which it was established. The existence of these divisions within the Irish republican movement was to assume great significance in the years that lay ahead. Many republicans, it is true, belonged to more than one organization, but the risk of conflicting loyalties and attitudes was inherent in the situation.

This danger of division and of possible confusion of aims reflected the changes which had taken place in the structure of Irish politics between 1914 and 1917. The I.R.B. had made the Volunteers an instrument not of Home Rule agitation but of republican revolution, yet Sinn Féin remained in an ambiguous position as a political party until 1917 and even then, as we have seen, more than a hint of compromise still remained on the constitutional issue. The meeting of the first Dáil, in

January 1919, did not resolve the difficulties. As a part of its policy of defying the British Government in every field of administration, Dáil Éireann set up its own cabinet under a Priomh Aire, Mr. de Valera, and the new government included a ministry of defence. What was to be the relationship between that ministry, headed by Cathal Brugha, and the Volunteers? This was an important question especially as the British threat to extend conscription to Ireland and the arrests following the so-called German Plot had provoked not merely a great deal of concern and anger but had helped to swell the ranks of the Volunteers. Again, the setting up, in Dublin, of a G.H.Q., in March 1918, strengthened the efficiency of the force and made possible some measure of systematic military planning.

In 1919, the Volunteers and the Dáil already had considerable public backing, but the two remained independent of one another. Far more evidence must be made available before historians can assess with any confidence the exact relations between the Volunteers and the Dáil in 1919, but certain trends seem clear enough. Some leaders of the Volunteers, for instance, had never been members of the I.R.B., others, for various reasons, had left the Brotherhood. Cathal Brugha wanted the army to be controlled directly by the Dáil ministry and freed from the influence of the I.R.B. Brugha and others distrusted the I.R.B. They saw it as a secret society and they may have suspected its leaders of pursuing policies not approved by Dáil Éireann. And they may have regarded the traditional methods of the Brotherhood as being too devious. It seems that the Priomh Aire, Mr. de Valera, shared Brugha's attitude in urging that the Volunteers should surrender their independence and become the armed forces of Dáil Éireann. In contrast, Michael Collins, already a leading figure in both the I.R.B. and the Volunteer executive, had reservations about bringing the army completely under the control of the Dáil—apparently on the grounds that it would be unwise to submit military decisions to any outside civilian authority.

The human factor, the temperamental differences and personal rivalries that existed between Brugha and Collins sharpened the conflict, but the primary issue remained whether or not the Volunteers should retain their autonomy, an autonomy which indirectly strengthened the influence of the I.R.B.

On April 10, 1919, Mr. de Valera told the Dáil that 'the minister of national defence is of course in close association with the voluntary military forces which are the foundation of the national army'—a carefully worded declaration which indicated that the Volunteers, at this stage, were associated with rather than subordinate to the Dáil ministry. It was not, in fact, until much later in the year that serious steps were taken to draw the Volunteers more firmly within the jurisdiction of Dáil Éireann.

On August 20, 1919, Brugha proposed a significant resolution in the Dáil. He asked that all Dáil deputies and all members of the Volunteers should take the same oath of allegiance to the state. The essential clause in the oath was that every deputy and volunteer should undertake to 'support and defend the Irish Republic and the Government of the Irish Republic, which is Dáil Éireann, against all enemies, foreign and domestic, and I will bear true faith and allegiance to the same'. The minister argued that it was only fair that the deputies should take the initiative in this matter and accept the oath before asking the Volunteers to do so. In making this suggestion, he had the enthusiastic support of Arthur Griffith, then the acting president of Dáil Éireann and, in effect, the acting head of the state. After a brief debate, the Dáil gave its approval to the new oath.

The Volunteer executive, it would seem, had already agreed to recommend acceptance of the oath by the next Volunteer convention, and this decision was undoubtedly a considerable concession to Brugha and his friends. But it was far from clear what practical limitations the taking of the oath would impose on the independence of the Volunteer movement, and it proved impossible, because of the danger of the delegates being arrested, to summon a delegate convention to make the necessary changes in the constitution of the Volunteers. Instead, the representatives of the local units were invited to signify their approval or disapproval of the oath and the majority of them appear to have accepted it eventually.

In terms of strict procedure, the Volunteers never ratified the change in their status, never made the necessary alterations in their constitution, and this was to be of some importance in the tangled arguments and controversies that followed the split on the Treaty. Despite the oath, the Volunteers seem to have remained in many ways very much an autonomous force. G.H.Q. increased its control over the local units and I.R.B. men continued to hold many of the key posts. Michael Collins, for example, was minister for finance in the Dáil cabinet and president of the Brotherhood and he held, in addition, the important military offices of director of intelligence and adjutant-general of the Volunteers.

The creation of the Dáil ministry of defence and the rather informal steps taken to bring the Volunteers under the Dáil's authority prompt certain questions. To what extent, for instance, did the Volunteer G.H.Q. reach policy decisions in relation to military operations or the purchase of arms independently of the Dáil ministry? It is known that the southern military leaders, especially Liam Lynch, played an important part in urging headquarters to intensify planned attacks on Royal Irish Constabulary barracks and British military installations in order to secure arms. To what extent these operations were undertaken independently of the republican government remains an open question. It looks as if military policy, in 1919–20, was left very much to the leaders of the Volunteers. While obviously many incidents and raids took place without the consent of the Dublin headquarters, the surviving Collins's papers leave the impression that the headquarters' staff kept a reasonably close grip over the major actions in the provinces, a remarkable feat considering the difficult circumstances under which the Volunteers had to operate.

I do not propose to examine here the struggle which the Volunteers conducted against the Crown forces in 1920–21. But some aspects of it must be considered. In the closing weeks of 1919 and into 1920, the Volunteers' military campaign was essentially a guerrilla one directed mainly against the R.I.C. Occasionally it took the form of a bold gesture such as the attempted ambush of Lord French. Again, the elimination of spies and informers absorbed much of the attention of the Volunteers' intelligence service in 1920. It would contribute much to our knowledge of the period if we could determine the extent to which consultations took place between the cabinet, the ministry of defence and the Volunteer headquarters. Collins and Brugha, in their different ways, provided some link between the Dáil cabinet and the army, but the nature of the links, even the routine ones, remains exceedingly obscure. It is certainly striking that it was not until a late date in the Anglo-Irish conflict that the Dáil, on March 11, 1921, formally endorsed the actions of the army and even then it did so in a rather unusual, almost circumspect manner.

The difficulties of building up a normal pattern of government were increased by the British decision to declare the Dáil an illegal body, compelling the republican parliament and its departments to conduct their business as best they could in semi-secrecy. But the problem of the relations between the combatant organizations was at least simplified by one decision taken by the I.R.B. As late as 1919, the I.R.B. had apparently considered its president as being in fact as well as by right, president of the Irish Republic. The constitution of the Brotherhood was amended, it would seem, to enable I.R.B. men to accept the new oath of allegiance to the Dáil, which was described as 'a duly elected public authority competent to declare the will' of the Irish people and established through the policy of the I.R.B. Significantly, too, the claim of the president of the I.R.B. to be the president of the republic was also dropped, but the Brotherhood was not dissolved; it simply accepted the Dáil as the legislative authority in the state. In the circumstances, it was not inappropriate that Michael Collins, the head of the I.R.B., should have become acting president of the Dáil when Griffith was arrested in November 1920.[1]

The bitterness of the Black-and-Tan war, the burning of Cork City, in December 1920, and the 'pogroms' in Ulster, may have prompted the makers of military policy to depart from their usual pattern of guerrilla warfare and attempt to deliver a more ambitious blow against the British. The burning of the Custom House, Dublin, in May 1921, was a major

[1] Griffith had been appointed acting president while Mr. de Valera was in America in connection with the republican loan campaign.

F

undertaking aimed at paralysing a part of the British administrative system. It was costly in terms of manpower, but it was
an action launched, it seems, with the approval of the cabinet.
If it represented the tentative beginnings of a new military
policy based on more open warfare, then it would be useful to
know to what extent it reflected a general departmental or
cabinet decision, but the truce of the summer of 1921 effectively
prevented any further changes in the nature of the conflict
between the Volunteers and the British forces.

At the first meeting of Dáil Éireann in 1919, a 'Message to
the free nations of the World' was adopted. In it mention was
made of 'the existing state of war between Ireland and England',
but surprisingly at no time in 1919 or 1920 did Dáil Éireann
make a formal declaration of war on Great Britain although it
did vote funds to finance the Volunteers. Its support, therefore,
for the specific military actions taken by the Volunteers was
more implicit than explicit. This reticence, even if largely
accidental, was open to the obvious criticism that it could
strengthen the impression that the army and the Dáil still
continued to go their own ways. Mr. de Valera, on his return
from America, soon raised the war issue and the question of the
Dáil's accepting full responsibility for what the Volunteers had
done. His initial statement to the Dáil, on March 11, 1921, and
his intervention in the subsequent debate throw useful light on
the uncertainties of the position as late as the spring of 1921.
'He did not think,' he told the House in a private session, 'that
their men should appear to be in the position of working as
irresponsible forces' and he considered it 'absolutely necessary
that the Dáil should let the world know that they took full
responsibility for all the operations of their army. That would
practically mean a public acceptance of a state of war. He did
not think there had been such formal acceptance up to the
present.'

In the debate the same day on the public acceptance of a
state of war with Britain, Mr. de Valera again made the point
that the Dáil 'was hardly acting fairly by the army in not
publicly taking full responsibility for all its acts'. On balance,
the president of the Dáil felt that the members should accept

a state of war and they could then instruct their consuls abroad
to seek belligerent rights for the republic. The question before
the Dáil was not one involving a new declaration of war but
rather a definite acceptance of responsibility for the warlike
actions that had already taken place.

The deputies, after some debate, agreed that the president
should be empowered to draw up a statement on the lines he
had indicated and 'that this be done at whatever time was
considered most opportune'. The opportune time came at the
end of March. In a press statement, Mr. de Valera announced
that the 'army is . . . a regular state force, under the civil control
of the elected representatives . . . and under officers who hold
their commissions under warrant from these representatives.
The government is, therefore, responsible for the actions of this
army.'

The available evidence suggests that this belated parliamentary decision of March 1921 may have helped to some extent to
strengthen the links between the Dáil and the army. It left
unresolved the problem of who should, in practice, take policy
decisions—the ministry or the army leadership. Despite the
changes made in the constitution of the I.R.B., there was much
disagreement, in the summer and autumn of 1921, on the question of the Brotherhood's influence within the army. Collins's
position was a formidable one, a number of important G.H.Q.
officers were I.R.B. men and another member of the Brotherhood, Richard Mulcahy, was chief of staff. The wider issue still
remained of whether or not the I.R.B. should continue to be
regarded as the guiding force in Irish republicanism.

The treaty negotiations dominated Irish politics throughout
the closing months of 1921. Hostilities were officially suspended
but there was the possibility that, should the London talks
break down, the British would launch a massive military assault
against the Volunteers. To meet any such danger, Mr. de Valera
and Brugha appear to have pressed for a reorganization of the
army and it was urged that the opportunity should be taken to
bring the army under the effective control of the Dáil executive.

There is some evidence to suggest that Brugha, in 1921,
sought without success to remove Collins from his post of

director of intelligence, but it was in October and November 1921 that the question about the control of the army became a really urgent one. In October, the Dáil cabinet decided in favour of a reorganization of the army. New commissions, issued under the authority of the Dáil Government, were to be offered to serving officers and the oath of allegiance to the republic and the government was to be readministered to the whole force. The constitutional subordination of the army to the Dáil having been asserted, the way would then be free for possible new appointments to military commands and to the G.H.Q. staff.

The history of the 'New Army' interlude is by no means complete, but it would seem that the turning point came with a joint meeting of the cabinet and G.H.Q. staff on November 25. Members of the staff were dissatisfied with the government's scheme and with the proposal that Eoin O'Duffy, a member of the Supreme Council of the I.R.B., should be removed from the office of deputy chief of staff. The government's plan was dropped and the signing of the Articles of Agreement—the Treaty—in London, on December 6, quickly changed the whole military situation in Ireland.

In the alignment of interests during October and November could, perhaps, be seen a foreshadowing of the subsequent division of parties over the Treaty. The weight of I.R.B. opinion at Supreme Council and G.H.Q. level had been against the government's military proposals while Brugha and his friends had favoured them. Later, in December and January, the majority of the I.R.B. Supreme Council were to come out in support of the Treaty, just as Brugha and de Valera, in their different ways, were to be counted among its most vigorous critics. It would be wrong to press the parallels between the two disputes too far as many new factors came into play in shaping the rival parties inside and outside Dáil Éireann on the Treaty issue. Liam Lynch, for example, could disapprove of the government's 'New Army' plan and yet break with the majority of his fellow members of the I.R.B. Supreme Council on the question of accepting or rejecting the Treaty. The Treaty dispute did not have its origins in the army controversy as such, but that half-hidden problem did help to heighten the tensions and, perhaps, to define more clearly the contending parties in the great and bitter struggle that lay ahead.

Before the end of the year 1921 there were already signs of a new and in some ways surprising turn in the old dispute between the friends of army independence and the Dáil. On December 12, 1921, the Supreme Council of the I.R.B. issued a statement which said: 'The Supreme Council having due regard to the constitution of the organization has decided that the present peace treaty between Ireland and Great Britain should be ratified. Members of the organization, however, who have to take public action as representatives are given freedom of action in the matter.' The I.R.B. Supreme Council, it would seem, was prepared to accept the Treaty as a 'stepping stone' to an internationally recognized Irish Republic. They had found common cause with the pro-Treaty majority in the Dáil and they could argue that their decision was in accord with the Brotherhood's policy of making use of 'all instruments political and otherwise' to achieve full national independence. But in doing so they helped to create a new political situation. From this time onwards it was the enemies of the Treaty who were to find in the notion of an autonomous Volunteer executive a potent weapon with which to challenge the plans of Collins, the majority of the members of the Supreme Council of the I.R.B. and the pro-Treaty party in Dáil Éireann.

The right of the army to act independently of the Dáil was boldly asserted by the new anti-Treaty army executive, on March 28, 1922, when it was announced that 'from this date neither the minister of defence nor his chief of staff shall exercise any control over the army'. A number of the arguments advanced by the anti-Treaty Volunteers to justify their defiance of the Dáil ministry must have sounded strangely familiar to some of their opponents who had to answer them.

7

PARTITION: THE ULSTER QUESTION (1916–1926)

By Maureen Wall

THE EASTER RISING of 1916 was as much a revolt against the Irish Parliamentary Party as against British rule in Ireland. It was already clear, after the 'Curragh Mutiny' and the Buckingham Palace conference in 1914, that the party policy of relying on the Liberals to achieve Home Rule for Ireland had failed. The power of the House of Lords had been broken, and Home Rule had reached the statute book, but the Liberals were neither able nor willing to enforce it in face of Ulster's continued resistance. From this time on Liberals and Tories were beginning to agree on partition as a possible compromise solution, and for the last four years of his life John Redmond, no longer holding the balance of power, continued to struggle for Irish unity, with the knowledge that Ulster Unionism could now rely on the backing of both English parties, and with the knowledge too that his leadership was being seriously questioned by Irish Nationalists. Hope deferred and the threat of a divided Ireland, would soon turn Home Rulers into republicans. Padraig Pearse, who had spoken with Redmond on a Home Rule platform in Dublin in 1912, and who, as late as January 1914, referred to the Volunteers as a weapon to assist Redmond to enforce Home Rule, was to head the provisional government which proclaimed an Irish Republic.

Redmond, who had underestimated the strength of anti-British feeling in Dublin, just as for years he had underestimated

79

the strength of anti-Home Rule feeling in Belfast, had pursued a policy of co-operating fully in the British war effort, hoping thereby to ensure general British support for Home Rule at the end of the war. But the rebellion showed the government that the policy of 'jam tomorrow' would no longer meet the critical Irish situation. The army could ill-afford the troops necessary to keep down disaffection in Ireland; recruiting there had virtually dried up, and above all, Irish-American pressure might prove an obstacle to the hoped-for entry of the United States into the war. Asquith, the prime minister came on a fact-finding mission to Ireland, and on his return, announced that Lloyd George, minister of munitions, had been entrusted with the task of bringing Home Rule into operation at once.

From this time until the signing of the treaty, Lloyd George was to be the chief negotiator on the British side in Anglo-Irish discussions, and his attitude to the problem did not change fundamentally during the five years between 1916 and 1921. He regarded partition as probably the only practicable basis for a settlement, but he also realized that the points of view of Unionists and Nationalists, which had emerged during the Buckingham Palace discussions, could prolong the Home Rule controversy indefinitely, and the Irish question would continue to occupy the time and attention of the British Parliament, and prove a stumbling block to Anglo-American understanding. If the minister of munitions were to be enabled to get on with his chief task of winning the war, it was urgently necessary to get the Irish question off the agenda, by means of an interim settlement, which would paper over the cracks for the time being, at least.

Thus, he got Carson to agree to ask his followers in Ulster to drop their opposition to Home Rule, provided the six counties of Antrim, Down, Armagh, Derry, Tyrone and Fermanagh, were excluded from its operation. There was to be no return to the bickering over bits of counties which had characterized the Buckingham Palace Conference. It must, Carson insisted, be a clean cut of six counties, and it must be permanent, for Ulster would never accept a sentence of death with a stay of execution. Lloyd George appears to have convinced Redmond, on the other hand, that partition was to be only a provisional solution. Nevertheless, Carson had in his possession when he arrived in Ulster, a letter from Lloyd George, which prominent Ulster Unionists regarded as a pledge that the excluded counties would never be forced to merge with the rest of Ireland. Because of their faith in this assurance and in view, they said, of the critical wartime situation, the Ulster Unionist Council agreed to the proposals, which meant the sacrifice of the Unionists of the rest of Ireland, and particularly of the convenanters in the counties of Donegal, Cavan and Monaghan.

Redmond, realizing that the leaders of the parliamentary party must show some results, or abdicate in favour of Sinn Féin, made an all-out effort to have the proposals accepted. His summary of Lloyd George's terms, which implied that partition would continue only for the period of the war and for a short time afterwards, was accepted by his parliamentary followers. But would the Northern Nationalists accept it? That was the real problem. A convention of Nationalists from the six counties met in Belfast on June 25, 1916. Under pressure from the A.O.H. and faced with the threat of Redmond's resignation the convention reluctantly consented to partition as a 'temporary and provisional settlement of the Irish difficulty' by 475 votes to 265.

When discussions began in parliament, however, on legislation to put Lloyd George's proposals into effect, government speakers made it clear that there would be no question of the automatic inclusion of Ulster in the Home Rule scheme at some future date. This could only be effected, if ever, by special act of parliament. Ulster Unionists could be well satisfied with what was in effect a public pledge that they would not be coerced. If that was to be the meaning of a 'temporary and provisional settlement' Redmond's supporters would have none of it, and the rising tide of indignation in Ireland, particularly among Ulster Nationalists, left him no option but to withdraw his assent to Lloyd George's proposals. Lloyd George's first attempt to achieve a settlement by the method of running with the hare and hunting with the hounds had failed, and Home Rule was dropped once again.

From time to time the suggestion had been made that Irishmen themselves should try to find an agreed solution on the lines of that achieved by the Land Conference of 1902. This idea was taken up by the government in the spring of 1917. America's entry into the war, early in April, had made it more than ever essential to put Irish affairs on a satisfactory footing, to ensure harmonious relations between the new allies. In May, Lloyd George proposed to Redmond that a Convention of Irishmen of all parties, should be summoned, to seek a settlement and to draft a Constitution for the country.

The Convention, which assembled on July 25, 1917, represented so many diverse interests, that it would have been humanly impossible for it to have arrived at an agreed solution. It included government nominees, members of the Irish Parliamentary Party, local government representatives, Ulster Unionists and Southern Unionists, Catholic and Protestant bishops, peers, business interests and representatives of labour. Sinn Féin were allocated five seats but they refused to attend, and although Ulster Unionists attended they contributed nothing to the efforts to reach agreement. They entered the Convention secure in the knowledge that the government would never coerce them if they continued to adopt a 'not an inch' stand. In the circumstances a compromise solution was impossible. The Convention adjourned in April 1918. From the government point of view it had been successful. It had given the impression abroad that Irishmen were being encouraged to settle their own affairs, and for almost a year a decision could be safely postponed.

John Redmond had died in March 1918 and the Irish Party was virtually wiped out in the general election of that year. Those of the sixty-nine Sinn Féin members elected, who were not in prison or 'on the run' set up an Irish Government in Dublin in January 1919. But Dáil Éireann was in itself a demonstration of the cleavage which existed in the Irish population, for all but three of its members were Catholics, and even these three can hardly be said to have represented a large body of Protestant voters. The twenty-six Unionists elected in 1918, apart from one Dublin and two Trinity College members, were all returned for Ulster constituencies, and they continued to attend parliament in Westminster.

The Dáil at once declared itself the Government of the Irish Republic, thereby re-stating the whole problem of Anglo-Irish relations. As was to be expected, an Irish Republic proved no more attractive to Ulster Unionists than Home Rule had done.

By the end of 1919, however, it was becoming increasingly evident that the pre-war Home Rule Act was now hopelessly out of date, and the British government introduced a new bill for the Government of Ireland early in 1920. Against a background of rising tension, with military and Black-and-Tan activity in Ireland, the bill passed slowly through its various stages, becoming law in December 1920. It provided for the setting up of two governments in Ireland, one in Belfast for the six counties of Northern Ireland, and the other in Dublin for the twenty-six counties of what was to be called Southern Ireland, though it would include Donegal, the most northerly county of all.

Ostensibly aiming at the ultimate unification of Ireland, or at least at a federal solution, section 2 of the Act provided for a Council of Ireland, which would bring about harmony between the two governments and administer certain services affecting the whole country. Although the new act was, in many ways, a great advance on previous Home Rule measures, it had come too late, and was entirely unacceptable to Dáil Éireann. Indeed no group in Ireland was enthusiastic about the Government of Ireland Act: Ulster Unionists regarded it, they said, as the 'supreme sacrifice', though it is true that they soon became very attached to the settlement, which can best be described as Unionist Home Rule, despite the seeming contradiction in terms. Nationalists in the six counties still hoped for union with the South, but in the meantime they would have preferred government from Westminster, while Southern Unionists were naturally opposed to partition which left them a tiny minority in the twenty-six counties.

But the setting up of a separate government for Northern Ireland as a first step in solving the Irish problem, led, as Lloyd George must have known it would, to the creation of vested interests which would tend to strengthen the case for permanent partition. In May 1921 a meeting was arranged between Sir James Craig, who was to head the government of Northern Ireland, and Mr. de Valera, president of Dáil Éireann, but the meeting was unsuccessful. The Council of Ireland, in which Craig professed himself willing to co-operate, if the South were to accept the Government of Ireland Act, was never set up, and a system of boycotting of Belfast goods, approved by Dáil Éireann, did nothing to improve relations between the two parts of Ireland, or between Unionists and Nationalists in the north-east.

Elections under the Government of Ireland Act took place in May 1921, forty Unionists being returned in the six north-eastern counties as against twelve Nationalists and Republicans. The Northern Ireland Parliament was officially opened by King George V in June, and opponents of partition were presented with a *fait accompli*. The king's speech foreshadowed a more conciliatory Irish policy, but it held no promise of a republic, or even of all-Ireland Home Rule, except with the consent of the new parliament of Northern Ireland. Nevertheless, within a few days peace negotiations were under way, and the British Government, having disposed of the Ulster problem, now proceeded to negotiate an Anglo-Irish settlement with the representatives of Dáil Éireann.

The only part of the treaty negotiations which interests us here is that part which relates to partition. The Dáil was still resolutely opposed to partition, although it was willing to consider local autonomy for the six counties under an all-Ireland Parliament. In August 1921, during the preliminary negotiations, Mr. de Valera had stated that Sinn Féin did not propose to use force to settle the Ulster question. So to all the other pledges collected down the years since 1912, Ulster Unionists could now add one from Dáil Éireann, guaranteeing that they would not be coerced into joining a united Ireland.

During the treaty discussions Lloyd George wrote several letters to Sir James Craig, proposing Irish unity, and guaranteeing adequate securities to the Unionists, but the attitude of the Government of Northern Ireland was, 'what we have we hold' and they refused to take any part in discussions which did not begin with the acceptance of that proviso. The British negotiators sympathized with the viewpoint of the Irish delegates, but not to the extent of coercing the Northern Ireland Government, and the two constant factors which had prevented a settlement ever since 1912—northern intransigence, and British unwillingness to apply coercion to the Unionists in that part of Ireland—would once again have brought about a stalemate, but for the diplomatic skill of the prime minister. The achievement of a speedy settlement was his main object, and he succeeded by by-passing the Ulster rock on which so many promising negotiations had already perished. By adroit manoeuvering in the last stages of the negotiations, he managed to persuade Arthur Griffith that he was in honour bound to stand by the terms of a document embodying a solution of the northern Ireland problem, which had been submitted to him privately, early in November. This piece of sharp practice prevented the Irish delegates from breaking off the negotiations on the question of Ulster, as had been their intention all along, if the talks should prove unsuccessful. In the event a treaty was signed, whereby the representatives of Dáil Éireann reluctantly agreed to accept dominion status instead of the republic they had fought for, while the Unionists in Northern Ireland were left entirely free to vote themselves out of the new dominion, and perpetuate the partition already effected by the Government of Ireland Act of 1920. But the Irish delegates were evidently persuaded that this partition would be of short duration, and that force of circumstances would soon compel Northern Ireland to join the Free State.

Lloyd George had failed to effect a settlement in 1916 because the conflicting interpretations of his proposals for agreement had been revealed during the debates in parliament. But in 1921 he succeeded on the basis of a package deal. The treaty was first signed. The interpretations of its clauses would come later. It is surprising that the Irish delegates, particularly Griffith, who had always evinced a keen interest in Irish history, should not have been mindful of the fact that the last occasion on which English and Irish negotiators had met to draw up articles of agreement, had been at the time of the surrender at Limerick in 1691, and accordingly paid particular attention to the wording of the document they were being asked to sign.

Reading the articles of agreement today, simply as a historical document, one is struck by the fact that the implementation of the articles relating to Northern Ireland depended on the co-operation of the Northern Ireland Government, which was not a party to the agreement at all, just as in 1691, the implementation of the articles of Limerick had rested largely with the Irish Parliament, which had taken no part in the negotiations.

The articles provided for local autonomy for the North, if the government there chose to remain in the Irish Free State. If, however, the Northern Ireland Government opted out, then a boundary commission would be set up to determine the boundary between Northern Ireland and the rest of the country. This commission would consist of a representative for Northern Ireland, a representative for the Irish Free State and a representative for the British Government, who would act as chairman. The Irish delegates seem to have believed that the Boundary Commission would award to the Free State some or all of the following areas: Fermanagh, Tyrone, South Armagh, Derry City and Newry, which were predominantly Nationalist, and that the area left under the jurisdiction of the Northern Ireland parliament would be so restricted that it would prove to be an uneconomic unit and would very soon beg for incorporation in the Irish Free State. But, although Lloyd George, Churchill, Birkenhead and the other British signatories deliberately encouraged the Irish delegates in this optimistic view of the possibilities of the Boundary Commission, there is nothing in the words of the article to justify that optimism, and in the long run it was words which mattered.

First, the commission was to determine the boundaries 'in accordance with the wishes of the inhabitants', but nothing was laid down as to the areas, whether counties, parishes or electoral divisions, within which enumeration of the inhabitants would take place. Secondly, the 'wishes of the inhabitants' were to be considered only 'in so far as may be compatible with economic and geographic conditions', a qualifying phrase which could be used to override the will of the inhabitants of almost any area, depending on the views of the Commissioners. Lastly, the Irish delegates seemingly assumed that the British-nominated chairman would automatically support any adjustment of the boundary which would favour the Free State. It is quite clear, however, from the debates in the British Parliament on the Irish Agreement Act early in 1922, that Unionists there did not believe that any substantial change in the existing border was contemplated, or they would not have agreed to the treaty so readily.

It is astonishing to find so little attention paid to the Ulster question in the printed reports of the debates which took place in Dáil Éireann between the signing of the treaty and its adoption by a majority of the Dáil on January 7, 1922. Of 338 pages of debate, nine only are devoted to the subject of partition, and of these nine pages the deputies for county Monaghan, deputies Blythe, MacEntee and O'Duffy, contributed two thirds. Collins, who represented Armagh in the Dáil, asserted that the treaty had made an effort to deal with the question of north-east Ulster on lines, which in his opinion, would 'lead very rapidly to good-will, and the entry of the north-east under the Irish Parliament'. 'If', he added, 'our policy is as has been stated, a policy of non-coercion, then let somebody else get a better way out of it.' Griffith made no reference at all to article twelve.

Critics of the treaty concentrated on the crown, the oath and the empire, for the most part, and several of those who did make a fleeting reference to the Northern Ireland question, were concerned not with the loss of the six counties, but rather with the fact that this part of Ireland could provide a bridgehead when Britain decided to re-establish her rule in Ireland. Indeed document number 2—the alternative proposal put forward by Mr. de Valera—showed no alteration in the articles relating to Northern Ireland, and seems to indicate that President de Valera had been convinced by the delegates that the Boundary Commission would solve the problem of partition. Neither side had a better solution to offer, and the formula of the Boundary Commission was not scrutinized too minutely, as far as is known.

It is interesting to speculate on what might have happened, had Dáil Éireann remained united in 1922. Had a united Dáil rejected the treaty, they might have ultimately achieved an Irish Republic for the twenty-six counties, but any change in the position of Northern Ireland would have been very unlikely. Had a united Dáil accepted the treaty, the problem of reconciling Irish unity with non-coercion of Ulster would have remained as insoluble as ever. And it is of course not certain that a united Dáil would have been able to control the army.

The uncertainty of the position after the adoption of the treaty led to increasing tension in Northern Ireland, with rioting and violence and a great many deaths; while serious clashes between British forces and the I.R.A. occurred along the border. In these incidents pro-treaty and anti-treaty groups acted together, and as late as May 1922, Collins, without the knowledge of his colleagues Griffith and O'Higgins, was a party to supplying arms for use by northern divisions. But the outbreak of civil war in June 1922 brought such co-operation to an end, and the problem of partition was to a great extent lost sight of until hostilities ceased in April 1923. Indeed it could be argued that the outbreak of civil war prevented an even more serious conflict between Nationalists and Unionists, with all the frightful implications of a sectarian war, and the extension of the Belfast pogroms to the whole Northern Ireland area.

In December 1922 Northern Ireland opted out of the Free State and as soon as the civil war was over the Free State Government began to press for the establishment of the Boundary Commission. Northern Ireland refused to co-operate, and eventually in 1924 the treaty was amended to enable the British Government to appoint a representative to act for Northern Ireland. The Commission, consisting of Eoin Mac-Neill, for the Free State, J. R. Fisher, a prominent Belfast Unionist for Northern Ireland, and Justice Feetham of the South African supreme court representing the British Government, met for the first time in November 1924, Justice Feetham acting as chairman. For almost a year it pursued its task, examining maps and documents, interviewing witnesses and surveying the border area. The Commissioners had agreed to maintain a strict secrecy, and the Free State Government knew nothing of what was being decided until information was leaked to the press and the *Morning Post*, early in November 1925, published a forecast of the Boundary Commission Report. From this it appeared, that, apart from some slight frontier rectifications, the chief result of the deliberations of the commission was the award of an extensive area of East Donegal to Northern Ireland.

Eoin MacNeill's resignation from the commission soon afterwards was taken as proof that the forecast had been substantially correct. Had the other Commissioners presented the report, as they were entitled to do, the territorial changes recommended in it would according to the treaty, have been binding. In order to forestall such a move, President Cosgrave and other Free State ministers crossed to London, where after consultation with Sir James Craig and with the British authorities, an agreement was signed on the December 3, 1925, revoking the powers conferred on the Boundary Commission. The report was never published. The 1920 boundary was to remain unchanged, and the powers of the Council of Ireland— that symbol of ultimate unity provided for in the Government of Ireland Act and in the treaty—were transferred to the Government of Northern Ireland.

Ambiguities were now at an end. This time the Unionists had got all that they wanted, and the agreement bore the signatures not only of British and Free State representatives, but, for the first time, the signatures also of the representatives of Northern Ireland. The agreement of 1925 made provision for meetings between the Northern and Irish Free State Governments, to consider matters of common interest, but although the Dublin Government of the time described the agreement as 'an instrument solemnly executed in friendship' that friendship was never translated into co-operation at government level. Indeed the 1925 agreement with its jettisoning of the boundary clause and the Council of Ireland arrangement, which had hitherto served to obscure the harsh realities of partition, was bound to weaken the position of the pro-treaty

G

Free State Government, and with the ultimate financial settlement, signed a few months later, did much to bring about it's overthrow. In the circumstances, any attempt to effect a close understanding between the two governments in Ireland could only serve to strengthen the appeal of the anti-treaty opposition, which now disclaimed all responsibility for partition. The promised meetings between the two governments did not take place.

Northern Nationalists refused to become reconciled to partition. The Unionist majority in Northern Ireland could continue to represent itself as a beleaguered garrison, encircled by enemy territory, ever on its guard against the Catholic Nationalist fifth column in its midst. Politics in Northern Ireland have continued to follow the sectarian pattern of Orange and Green, and the passage of centuries has done little to alter the terms of the original conflict.

It would be true to say that partition exists in Ireland today, chiefly because the province of Ulster has, since the seventeenth century, unlike the other three provinces, possessed a population in which Protestants of all classes, have formed a very large part. For several hundred years Ireland was governed on colonial lines, and Protestant monopoly and discrimination against Catholics produced the political results which segregation has produced in most colonies. There were indeed Catholic Unionists, ten times as many it was said in 1886, as there were Protestant Home Rulers. Nevertheless the wide extension of the franchise in 1884 had revealed the clear cut lines of division between the Catholics of Ireland who voted overwhelmingly for Home Rule, and the Protestants of Ireland mainly resident in Ulster, who voted against it. During the protracted discussions on the third Home Rule Bill however, the issue was confused by arguments from history. Nationalist leaders all subscribed to the ideal of the brotherhood of Irishmen as formulated by Tone and Davis. Davis's assertion that 'It matters not if at different shrines we pray unto one God', had become part of Nationalist political teaching. Protestant Ireland, however, was very clear that the shrine they had worshipped at had entitled them and their ancestors to a superior position in the community for hundreds of years, and they were not prepared to relinquish that position for one of equality, perhaps even of inferiority, under a Catholic dominated parliament in Dublin.

With the one exception of the United Irish movement of the 1790s (the decade which saw also the foundation of the Orange Order) the tradition of Irish Protestantism had been one of eternal vigilance against the Catholic majority. The annual celebration of the siege of Derry and the battle of the Boyne preserved the memory both of deliverance and of victory, and Bonar Law well knew how to use historical propaganda to the best advantage when he told the cheering crowds at Balmoral in 1912:

> Once again you hold the pass—the pass for the Empire. You are a besieged city, and you have closed your gates. The government by their parliament act have erected a boom against you, to shut you off from the help of the British people.

He was speaking the language of his hearers, as was Carson in the Ulster Hall in 1914, when he asked:

> Is our reward to be that we are to be turned outside the United Kingdom; that we are to be put in a degraded position in the Empire; and above all that we are to be handed over, bound hand and foot, to those who have ever been your majesty's enemies and ours?

It was to such talk that the rank and file of Irish Protestants responded, and not to pleas for the brotherhood of Irishmen. It was idle for Redmond to suggest that Protestants, who had been politically and socially estranged, not to say segregated from Catholics for centuries, should overnight accept his vision of:

> ... a self governing Ireland in the future, when all her sons, of all races and creeds, within our shores, will bring their tribute, great or small to the grand total of national enterprise, national statesmanship and national happiness.

Carson was, therefore, to a great extent correct when he accused Nationalists of never trying to 'win over Ulster' and of never trying to 'understand her position'. They persisted instead in quoting Tone, Davis, Mitchel and Parnell as spokesmen of Protestant Ireland, when in fact they had become almost exclusively the adopted spokesmen of Irish Catholic Nationalism.

It was not always easy to keep rank and file nationalists convinced of the brotherhood of Irishmen, particularly in face of the pogroms in the north-east, but the realists among their leaders were well aware that the problem could not be settled in their favour by force, so long as public opinion in Britain could be relied on to respond unquestioningly to the cry of 'Protestants and loyalists in danger'. Redmond's problem had been to prevent partition becoming a fact, and he was already dead when the Government of Ireland Act effected it in 1921. Dáil Éireann's task from then on was to undo a partition already in existence, and taking all the circumstances into account, the probability of success was remote.

When Redmond had first faced concrete proposals involving partition on the basis of county options in 1914, Arthur Griffith fulminated against the scheme in the pages of *Sinn Fein*, taking his stand on rigid theories of nationality, and insisting that 'Ireland is the sole proprietor of Ulster, and not the generations on Ulster ground'. 'No generation,' he insisted, 'has the right to barter or alienate any part of the national heritage.' Yet the county option proposals of 1914, had they been agreed to, would have produced roughly the same results as Griffith expected to accrue from the decisions of the Boundary Commission, when he signed the treaty in 1921. The failure of the Boundary Commission to achieve the promised results left the British Government open to the charge of sharp practice, and saved the faces of nationalists by exonerating them from the charge of having willingly relinquished their claim to the six north-eastern counties. Since then the policy of all political parties in the twenty-six counties on the question of partition has been the negative one of non-acquiescence. An agreed settlement at any time since 1912 could scarcely have failed to bring about a better understanding between north and south than exists at present, but no nationalist or republican states-man has been prepared to ask his party or the electorate to give him a mandate for such a settlement. If he did, he would probably pay the short term price of immediate political eclipse. In the unlikely event of his carrying his party with him he would certainly pay the long term price of going down in popular history as the man who bartered or alienated a portion of the national territory.

Note:
Since the above was written the heads of the governments of Northern Ireland and the Republic of Ireland have met on friendly terms and it is now easier to implement that part of the 1925 agreement which provided for meetings between the two governments to consider 'matters of common interest'.

8

THE PASSING OF THE IRISH PARLIAMENTARY PARTY (1916–1918)

By F. S. L. Lyons

H ISTORY DOESN'T, as a rule, spare many tears for the defeated, and in the recent past of Ireland the triumph of the republic has largely overshadowed the constitutional Home Rule movement which, for the forty years before 1916, had embodied the hopes and aspirations of the great majority of Irish Nationalists. Yet the revolution which began in Dublin in Easter Week should surely be viewed not only in the light of what it achieved, but of what it displaced. Or, to put it another way, we cannot fully appreciate the achievement until we realize what an enormous swing of the pendulum it represented.

To understand the magnitude of this change it is important to remember—what nowadays it is very hard to remember—the deep roots which the old parliamentary party had sunk in Irish life and its almost complete dominance over Irish politics. Most people in 1916 had grown up in the era of constitutional nationalism, they knew its history and they respected its current leaders—John Redmond, John Dillon and Joseph Devlin—as the heirs and maintainers of a great tradition. The party was extremely well organized and vastly experienced, and it could claim with justice that nearly every major reform in Ireland between 1886 and 1914 was traceable to its efforts. Above all,

95

in 1914, it had won what seemed its crowning triumph in placing the Home Rule Act on the statute-book, even though the stubbornness of Ulster Unionism and the onset of the war had left the position of Ulster, indeed even the definition of Ulster, for the future to decide.

Up to 1914, therefore, the party was still formidable. Yet even by then cracks had begun to appear in that impressive façade. It had never really recovered from the Parnell split and though reunited in 1900, it had subsequently been plagued by all kinds of dissensions and secessions. The really disastrous effect of the split, however, was that it alienated many of the young men who were reaching maturity during that fatal decade of the 1890s and who, in their revulsion from the party, were attracted towards other organizations of which the constitutional leaders took little or no account. Before the war these had no large following, and the turbid waters of Irish politics were much more rudely ruffled by Sir Edward Carson than by Sinn Féin, or the Gaelic League, or the Irish Volunteers, or the Citizen Army, or even the I.R.B. But the very success of Ulster Unionism in undermining the whole fabric of parliamentary government was a deadly blow to constitutional nationalism. Eoin MacNeill, calling on one occasion for three cheers for Carson, may have been too sophisticated for his audience, but there was nothing wrong with his logic.

The hard truth is that the great climax of 1914 degenerated, almost from the moment of its achievement, into anti-climax. Redmond's success was nullified partly by the failure to solve the Ulster question, but partly also by his generous, but politically dangerous, offer to the British Government on the outbreak of the war that they should withdraw all their troops from Ireland and leave the Irish to defend their own shores. Redmond had always tended to think imperially as well as nationally and the war intensified this trait in his character. He became emotionally involved in the struggle, and his anxiety that Ireland should contribute her share led him into a serious miscalculation of the way the tide was flowing at home. But although he and other members of the party did throw themselves into a recruiting drive for the army, the government did not co-operate, and the enthusiasm he had sought to kindle never caught fire. On the contrary, the identification of the party with recruiting was to be a damning item in the indictment which was soon to be drawn against it. Almost at once, indeed, this policy led to a split in the Volunteers and the passing of part of that body out of Redmond's control into the hands of those who were to use it as the nucleus of the force which was to strike the blow the I.R.B. had determined should be struck before the war was over.

When the explosion duly came in 1916 it took the party by surprise, and its immediate reaction was the characteristic reaction of middle class, conservative nationalism—horror and anger. But soon all was changed, changed utterly. The executions ordered by General Maxwell redoubled the horror and transformed the anger into pity. Such a revulsion of feeling in the country presented grave dangers to the parliamentary party, but of the triumvirate who ruled it—Redmond, Dillon and Devlin—only Dillon was in Dublin. His house was very close to the main scene of the fighting, and he was shut up there with his family throughout the whole rebellion. While appalled, as others were, by the destruction and loss of life during Easter Week, he had at once grasped the crucial fact of the situation— that if the government retaliated by shooting the leaders the effect on public opinion would be disastrous. His reactions did credit both to his head and to his heart. So long as he remained in Dublin he did everything he could to restrain the military authorities in their vengeance, and when at last in May 1916 he got to London he delivered in the House of Commons one of the most celebrated speeches of his career, declaring that those who had fought had fought a brave, clean fight, and launching a blistering attack upon the ineptitude of the government which had brought Ireland to such a pass.

The immediate consequence of the tragedy was one more attempt to reach a negotiated Irish settlement. Lloyd George, acting for a cabinet that was divided on the subject almost to the point of dissolution, offered immediate Home Rule to the twenty-six counties. Redmond believed that the exclusion of the six counties was only to be temporary, and on this under-

standing—though even then only after intense pressure—
persuaded northern nationalists to accept the arrangement for
the time being. Carson, who had his own difficulties with the
southern unionists, also accepted it, but to him Lloyd George
had written, 'we must make it clear that at the end of the
provisional period Ulster does not, whether she wills it or not,
merge in the rest of Ireland'. Even this, however, did not satisfy
the die-hard opponents of Home Rule whom Asquith dared
not offend lest, at this critical moment in the war, his cabinet
should break up altogether. Consequently, in July he announced
that once the six counties were excluded another act of parliament would be required to bring them in again, and the next
day that arch-unionist, Lord Lansdowne, declared bluntly that
exclusion was to be permanent. Redmond at once withdrew
his support and the whole scheme collapsed.

This curious and sordid episode had consequences far beyond
the immediate irritation it caused. Indeed, it turned out to be
a major crisis for the party. It created in Redmond's mind deep
distrust of Lloyd George, whom he always regarded as having
betrayed him—and this was particularly unfortunate since
Lloyd George was to be prime minister by the end of the year.
In Ireland the effect on public opinion was doubly disastrous.
On the one hand, the party was presented in the odious light
of having been prepared to barter the national unity for a
settlement which had apparently never even existed. And on
the other hand, the lifting of martial law, which had been
eagerly awaited as the first fruits of the agreement, did not
materialize, while the hanging of Casement in August revived
the bitterness aroused by the executions in May.

Finally, and most ominously, English opinion hardened
perceptibly. The losses of the Ulster division on the Somme were
contrasted with what to most Englishmen was the attempt to
stab England in the back with German aid, and it is not
surprising that talk of applying conscription to Ireland began
again to be heard. All the Irish party could do was to oppose
conscription and to demand the ending of martial law, the
recall of General Maxwell and the release of the hundreds of
interned suspects. And in fact in August the first of these began

to emerge—often more ardent Sinn Féiners than when they went in—in November the hated Maxwell was recalled, and in December more prisoners were allowed home, only the major figures still being kept in jail.

These relaxations, however, were due less to the party than to the need to placate American opinion. Irish-Americans had long been deeply divided, mainly between the moderate or Redmondite group and the Clan-na-Gael which, under John Devoy's guidance, had done so much to bring on the rising. The executions had caused intense anti-British feeling among both sections and, as the British ambassador in Washington reported, 'they have blood in their eyes when they look our way'. But by late 1916 the possibility of the United States entering the war was growing, and it became essential to conciliate the Irish-Americans in order to smooth the way for President Wilson, though from the British viewpoint his pronouncements about each people having the right to choose the sovereignty under which it should live made him an embarrassing ally.

It remained to be seen, however, whether this improvement would benefit the party or its opponents. Several crucial by-elections during 1917 answered this question decisively. The first was in North Roscommon, where the Sinn Féin candidate was Count Plunkett, an elderly, scholarly man whose chief claim to fame was that his son Joseph had been one of the executed leaders of the rising. He won the election easily and immediately declared that he would not take his seat at Westminster. It was possible to call this a freak result, the product of a wave of emotion, but in the inner circles of the Irish party it was taken much more seriously. Redmond, indeed, was so shaken that he drafted a manifesto for publication in which he sought to justify the party's record and to warn the country against the alternative policy its enemies were encouraged by the election to assert—separation from the Empire, withdrawal from Westminster, the establishment of a Republic, and the use of force, if need be, to achieve these aims. The country, he admitted, might well be tired of having been led by the same men for nearly forty years and he would not complain if replaced, but he ended by imploring his fellow-countrymen not to be led astray by passion into courses 'which must end in immediate defeat of their hopes for the present and permanent disaster to their country'.

Owing to the urgent demands of his closest colleagues Redmond did not publish this document, but that he should have written it at all, and in such a defeatist tone, after only one reverse at the polls, is striking evidence of how deeply infected by pessimism he had already become. Nor were the events of the succeeding months calculated to restore his confidence. In May, June and July three further by-elections were held and each was won by Sinn Féin—South Longford by Joseph McGuiness, East Clare by Mr. de Valera and Kilkenny by Mr. Cosgrave. In South Longford the party made an all-out effort, realizing how essential it was to wipe out the previous defeat at all costs. Dillon directed operations and from Longford he wrote bluntly to Redmond as follows: 'We have the Bishop, the great majority of the priests, and the mob—and four-fifths of the traders of Longford. And if in face of that we are beaten, I do not see how you can hope to hold the party in existence.' In the event they were beaten, and although the margin was only thirty-seven votes it was everywhere realized that the party had taken a long step towards oblivion.

Even more significant was the East Clare contest, caused by the death in action of the Irish leader's brother, Willie Redmond. It was significant because it was Mr. de Valera's first electoral battle and because, released from prison on the eve of the campaign, he clearly stated the issue as between republican separatism and constitutional Home Rule within the Empire. The party, so paralysed that it did not even select the candidate to oppose him, made a poor fight of it and Mr. de Valera's majority was decisive—he polled more than twice as many votes as his opponent.

This was the severest blow the party had yet received and not surprisingly signs of unrest and alarm began to spread through its ranks. Shortly after the Clare result had become known a letter or 'remonstrance' to Redmond was circulated amongst the members, though it was only signed by a tiny minority of them. It urged that the party policy in future should be based on the demand for full dominion status for Ireland and that if this were not conceded by Britain, then the demand should be made to the Allies, or even, ultimately, to the peace conference. The most curious feature of the document, however, was its ambivalent attitude towards Sinn Féin. Its authors declared that they could not accept the Sinn Féin doctrine of withdrawal from Westminster, still less that of separation from Britain which, they believed, would lead to a second rebellion, but they wrote fulsomely of their admiration 'for the aspirations which now stir the young men and women of Ireland.' 'We believe', they added, 'that the manifestation of their indomitable determination to win for Ireland her true place in the sun is the most hopeful sign of recent years.' In the light of subsequent events this remonstrance reads pathetically like an attempt to have a revolution without tears, but to Redmond himself it came as an ugly indication that he could not count indefinitely upon the unquestioning loyalty of a solidly united party.

While these important by-elections were being fought two major and closely connected events had changed the whole situation. The first was the entry of the United States into the war in April 1917. This had two effects upon the position in Ireland. On the one hand, those Sinn Féiners who took Wilson's remarks about self-determination for small nations at their face value, were encouraged in their determination to present the Irish case at the peace conference whenever it should come. And on the other hand it became more essential than ever for the British Government to take further steps to solve the Irish problem, so that Wilson might be freed from the embarrassment of Irish-American hostility to the war effort.

It was this consideration which produced the second new development of 1917—Lloyd George's attempt to reopen negotiations with the Irish leaders. The circumstances, however, were bleak enough. He could not move far towards Redmond without alarming the Unionists and even perhaps breaking up the cabinet, but if he did not move perceptibly he would not overcome Redmond's distrust, for, indeed, after 1916 the latter had sworn to have no more dealings with him.

The prime minister began on the old familiar tack by offering partition and, as was to be expected, got nowhere. Then he took up a suggestion which Redmond himself had made privately, and proposed that an Irish Convention, representative of all shades of opinion, should meet to hammer out an agreed solution. Such a Convention did meet in Trinity College in July, and continued to meet at intervals until the spring of 1918. But, although it gave an opportunity for moderate men on both sides to come together, it achieved virtually nothing, for two things damned it from the start. One was the inflexible attitude of the Ulster Unionists, and the other was that it was attended neither by Sinn Féin nor by organized labour. Any settlement reached in the absence of Sinn Féin would hardly have been worth the paper it was written on, but in fact such a settlement never came in sight.

While the Convention talked the government, as Dillon acidly remarked, seemed bent on 'manufacturing Sinn Féiners'. A running persecution of the leaders, or of people suspected of belonging to the movement, was kept up by the authorities, and although at first more exasperating than injurious, it became much more serious when some of those arrested began to go on hunger-strike. The death of Thomas Ashe under forcible feeding in September 1917 was a grim indication of what was always liable to happen in such circumstances and, from the government's viewpoint, was most serious, since Ashe had played a prominent part in the rising. His funeral was the occasion of a major demonstration and beyond question added fuel to the flames of resentment which had never really died down since the Maxwell régime.

Within a few weeks of this event a notable consolidation of the forces of militant nationalism took place at the annual Sinn Féin Convention in October. A few days before it was due to meet private and highly important negotiations were held between leading Republican and Sinn Féin representatives which resulted in broad agreement as to the lines on which the two movements were to act together. At the convention itself, after much debate, and on some issues very considerable differences of opinion, the original private agreement was confirmed, thus enabling Griffith's Sinn Féin movement and the Republicans to agree on the formula suggested by Mr. de Valera, which stated that Sinn Féin aimed at securing the international recognition of Ireland as an independent Irish Republic, but that having achieved that status the Irish people might by referendum freely choose their own government. At the same gathering Mr. de Valera was chosen as leader and since shortly afterwards he also became president of the Volunteers, it was clear where power was to be concentrated in the future. Republicans were strongly represented on the new Sinn Féin executive and, even more significantly, key positions in the Volunteers were occupied by members of the I.R.B.

As Sinn Féin grew in strength and organization, so too did the British Government increase its efforts to break it up by every device which the long history of repression had made familiar. Dillon later argued strongly that one motive for this policy—which of course only increased the hold of Sinn Féin on the country—was a deliberate desire by the authorities to ruin the Irish Parliamentary Party. In the sense that what happened in 1917 and 1918 cleared the ground for two opposite extremes to clash, with no room left for moderates, this was true enough. It is probably true also that with the failure of the Irish Convention to achieve anything concrete, the Irish party had already been largely written off by the government, the more so since the by-elections seemed to show that it no longer possessed the country's confidence. It could be argued, and some did argue, that since the party had actually won several con- tests between July 1917 and April 1918 life was far from extinct, but these victories were misleading, for they were all in seats where specially favourable circumstances prevailed, and events were soon to show that they were untypical. But, in any event, to assume that the policy of persecuting Sinn Féin was aimed at eliminating the party so that Irish nationalism could be exhibited to the outside world as irreconcilable, fanatical and thirsting for blood—and therefore to be crushed, not negotiated with, seems too Machiavellian. It is at least as possible that the government, recognizing that its adversary in the future would be Sinn Féin, not the party, determined to weaken that adversary as much as possible in advance, even if innocent bystanders like the parliamentarians got hurt in the process.

Partly, however, the tightening up was intended as a prelude to introducing conscription. This proposal came before parliament in April 1918, just a month after Redmond's death following an operation, and only a day after the Irish Convention had presented its ineffectual report. Dillon, who had succeeded Redmond as chairman of the party, at once led it out of the House of Commons and back to Ireland to organize resistance to this fresh threat. There then followed a most extraordinary display of national unity. On April 18 at a conference convened by the Lord Mayor in the Mansion House in Dublin, parliamentarians, Sinn Féin and labour sat round the table together and pledged themselves to resist conscription, a pledge that immediately received massive support from the Irish hierarchy which, meeting at Maynooth, denounced the measure as 'an oppressive and inhuman law', to be resisted 'by every means that are consonant with the laws of God'. This episcopal pronouncement was the more impressive since, despite the enthusiasm of a number of younger priests for Sinn Féin, the Church in general had so far looked with a very cold eye on the militant movement and was to do so again in the future.

The government, however, was prepared to use almost any weapon to force conscription through. Hence the fantastic episode of the 'German Plot'. On April 12 Joseph Dowling, a former prisoner in Germany and a member of Casement's Irish brigade, was rescued from an island off the coast of Galway. He was arrested, tried and sent to the Tower, and on the basis of this incident the government announced that Sinn Féin had been discovered to be in active touch with Germany in preparation for another insurrection. Immediately mass-arrests followed which swept into the net almost the entire Sinn Féin leadership, with, however, the exception of Michael Collins, whose key position in the later stages of the movement really derived from this time. No reasonable evidence was ever produced by the government to prove that the plot existed, but there is a certain irony in the fact that while Dowling did manage to convey a code message, it was Collins who received it. It is said to have been an assurance to the I.R.B. that if there *was* another rising, Germany would support it, but it seems that if any reply was made—and even this is doubtful—it was non-commital.

The arrests were the signal for intensified military rule in Ireland. Sinn Féin was officially suppressed (it continued to flourish unofficially, of course) and in many parts of the country public meetings of any kind were prohibited. Yet, the government still hesitated to take the irrevocable step of using force to impose conscription. Even this hesitancy, however, which might have relaxed the tension, in fact contributed to the worsening situation, for once the immediate threat had passed, the truce between the parliamentarians and Sinn Féin withered and died. It perished, to be precise, in the East Cavan by-election of May to June 1918, where Arthur Griffith, in prison again, like the other leaders, was put up by Sinn Féin and opposed by a party candidate. The contest was bitterly fought and Dillon himself went down to the constituency in a desperate last-minute attempt to retrieve the position. The policy of withdrawal from Westminster he denounced as 'a policy of lunatics'. As for the republic, 'we will not accept that' he said, 'as the object of the Irish movement'. He could not have been more emphatic. Neither could the electors of East Cavan who returned Griffith with a handsome majority.

East Cavan was in a sense a dress rehearsal for the general election which was now approaching fast. With the ending of the war in November, parliament was dissolved and in the following month the voters had their first opportunity for eight years to express their opinions *en masse* at the polls. The result is well known. Despite, no doubt partly because of, the fact that over 100 of its leading figures were in jail, Sinn Féin won a crushing victory. Out of 105 Irish seats they captured seventy-three, the Unionists twenty-six, and the parliamentary party, which in its prime had controlled as many as eighty-five, could only salvage six from the wreckage. Of these six, four in Ulster had been left to the party by agreement with Sinn Féin to avoid splitting the nationalist vote; one was in Waterford City, which remained unshakably loyal to the Redmond family, re-electing

H

John Redmond's son, after having put him in his father's seat only a few months earlier: and the last was in West Belfast, where the much-loved Joe Devlin succeeded in defeating Mr. de Valera. This achievement, however, was counter-balanced by the victory which Mr. de Valera won over John Dillon in East Mayo—a seat the latter had held for over thirty years.

That decision in East Mayo was symbolic. For when all the returns were in, it was universally realized that the old parliamentary party was dead without hope of resurrection. And when, on January 21, 1919, a new era opened in Ireland with the first meeting of Dáil Éireann, the tiny band of surviving constitutionalists was not present. This, after all, was only fitting. They had played their parts and it was time to go. Their tragedy was over. Another, vaster and far more bloody, was about to begin.

9

THE TREATY
NEGOTIATIONS

By Frank Pakenham

T HERE IS NO GAIN-SAYING the extraordinary change
which the Anglo-Irish Treaty brought to Ireland and her
relationship with Great Britain. The signature of this
document put a final close to the guerrilla war which had been
devastating Ireland from January 1919 when an Irish Republic
had been declared down to the truce of July 1921. Its deeper
consequence transformed the whole system under which Ireland
had previously been governed and the whole basis of Ireland's
relationship to England. The British supremacy over Ireland
first claimed in 1172 was virtually ended. The legislative union
that had linked the countries since 1800 was dissolved. Hitherto
Ireland had been one area among many within the United
Kingdom less independent than Scotland; administered from
Dublin Castle by a British Lord Lieutenant and a British Chief
Secretary, lacking since 1800 any legislator of her own. Just
before the war attempt had been made to give her a Dublin
Legislator strictly subordinate to Westminster, where a reduced
Irish representation would have continued and the attempt had
brought England within sight of civil war. Now Ireland attained
at a bound the status of a British Dominion and except as regards
naval and air defence (where the restrictions were removed
before the Second World War) the same degree of practical
independence. That was how I described the revolutionary
advance when I was writing my book about the Treaty, *Peace*

by Ordeal, which appeared in 1935. Against that, though this seems not to have been in my mind at the time, must be set the fact that Ireland, a united territory till the Partition Act of 1920, was from that time till now to be partitioned: twenty-six counties on one side of the line, six on the other.

Now we must distinguish between what was achieved, and the manner of its achievement.

It is theoretically possible that such a settlement could have been reached in the de Valera–Lloyd George discussion of July 1921 (as came about afterwards). The historic change would still have been tremendous, but the drama and tragedy which were the theme of my own book would have been greatly diminished, and the consequences very different for Ireland. On the one hand the civil war would have been averted; on the other hand the Irish people as a whole might have felt more morally bound by the settlement.

At any rate we are concerned with the story as it actually occurred with the attempt in the Autumn of 1921 to meet at the same time the Irish demand for independence and the British demand for security. At least that was felt to be the underlying issue. But in fact Mr. Lloyd George's invitation, accepted by Mr. de Valera to a Conference in October was phrased a little differently. He had refused to discuss any settlement which took Ireland outside the British Common-wealth but the actual words of his invitation were framed so as to leave the issue open. The Conference was to ascertain how the association of Ireland with the community of nations known as the British Empire might best be reconciled with Irish national aspirations. On September 30, Mr. de Valera accepted the invitation couched in these terms on the understanding that by coming into conference neither side was in any way committed to accepting the position of the other.

It is well known that Lloyd George who a year earlier was denouncing Irish nationality as a sham and a fraud and their military organization as 'a small body of assassins—a real murder gang', had in the course of the summer discussion already offer-ed Ireland the status of a dominion. The supreme achievement which emerged from the Treaty from the Irish point of view was already available, before the negotiations started, which is not to deny the improvement of the oath and the attainment of fiscal economy and other results of Irish bargaining.

It might be thought that three issues would overshadow all others. The status of the new Irish State; the unity or partition of Ireland; and the defence facilities claimed by Britain in the new Ireland. Looking back today one might have thought that the third question 'Defence' would have proved at least as thorny as any of the others. But in fact it was disposed of quite peaceably, although the use of the facilities in time of war might well have rendered it impossible for Ireland to remain neutral from 1939 to 1945; as it was Britain renounced the same facilities under the agreement in 1938.

The other two issues—Irish status and Irish unity—were central throughout and very much linked together in the tactics. The difference between the issues from the Irish point of view was simply this. In the circumstances of the time the British Government were bound to be strongly opposed to the constitutional status—outside the Commonwealth—which the Irish were demanding and about which I will speak in a few moments. But Lloyd George was able to carry his Cabinet with him, for a time at least, in seeking to promote the unity of Ireland without coercing the North, i.e. on this issue the two main parties were agreed at least on paper, while the Northern Government were the obstruction which it was hoped to overcome.

This situation led naturally to the deliberate and persistent Irish strategy throughout the Conference of trying 'to stage the break on Ulster'. The refinements of this idea and the tactical devices involved in it are explored at somewhat appalling length in my *Peace by Ordeal*. But the basic idea is easy to grasp. When the moment of decision arrived when Lloyd George would say to them, as in one form or another he was always likely to say to them, 'You come into the commonwealth, or else . . .' their strategy was to reply to him 'Not so fast please, Mr. Prime Minister. You tell us whether you are offering us a united or a partitioned Ireland. Until you can answer that question the world will back us up in refusing to answer your question whether we are prepared to give up the republic and become a dominion.'

Was this strategy sound in conception, assuming that the tactics to give effect to it had been adequate, i.e. much better than they were? I am more than doubtful myself whether in the last resort the strategy would have stood up in front of British or world opinion. It was surely bound to become recognized that this approval did not express a genuine readiness to come into the Commonwealth, even if the essential unity of Ireland were secured.

There appeared (in 1964) a new book by Lord Beaverbrook which includes many fascinating quotations from a diary kept by Lloyd George's private secretary during this period and other arresting material. After reading it, I feel that Lloyd George's internal position was weaker than I represented it as being in my book. Whether that means that the Irish position was stronger or otherwise is very much a matter of opinion. Be that as it may, there are two further thoughts on the subject of the 'break on Ulster'.

On page 213 of my book I find myself writing 'if there had been no 12[th of] November there might have been no Treaty'. That was the day when Arthur Griffith gave a personal pledge of some kind to Lloyd George which was put into writing and shown to him next day by Tom Jones and in some way accepted by him. The paper containing it was discovered by Lloyd George with some difficulty and brandished at Griffith with telling effect on the last afternoon of the conference and it altered the whole situation, the immediate situation at any rate.

I had forgotten until I looked up my book that the British had already withdrawn once on December 5, the last day, without much progress made before this paper was discovered and brandished. The Irish in the interval had already agreed that if the British insisted on an immediate answer they would break off negotiations, declining to sign or reject the terms pending a decision from Craig. They agreed also that whatever the exact nature of the predicament Griffith's last card should be to demand reference to the dominion premiers. In short the contingency of a demand for an immediate answer had already been covered in the Irish planning on the spot. Yet soon after the Conference resumed, when the paper is brandished at Griffith he shakes his pencil across the table and vehemently repudiates the charge that he might be breaking faith. 'I have never,' he insisted, 'let a man down in my whole life and I never will.' And then, but not till then, came his simple agreement to abandon all attempt to bring about the break on Ulster.

With that gone it is not surprising that Lloyd George soon felt the time ripe for the hammer stroke, the ultimatum, the historic threat of immediate and terrible war unless the Treaty was signed that day. I don't know whether I was the first; I have certainly not been the last to comment on the extraordinary neglect of the telephone line to Dublin.

But coming to it fresh today it seems to me that once Griffith had been personally induced to abandon the break on Ulster the chances were always great that he would agree to sign and that once he did so Collins, Duggan, and later Barton and Gavan Duffy would follow suit. And so it proved. Griffith responded to the ultimatum by saying immediately that he would sign even if no one else did. Collins gave out on the way back to the Irish Headquarters that he meant to sign. This astounded Barton. But from everything that we know now one would have been more astounded if Collins had separated himself from Griffith at this juncture, though I would not suppose that he would have urged signature unless Griffith had come out as he did. As it was he must have been very near the line. He knew and said that he was signing his death warrant. Churchill has said of him earlier that day that in all his life he had never seen so much pain and suffering in restraint. Duggan, Barton and Gavan Duffy agreed in due course—the last two after agonies of conscience.

I said a few minutes ago that the break on Ulster was a cock which probably wouldn't fight in the end; yet am I now saying that if Griffith had not been outsmarted on November 12 and 13 the Irish would have got away with it? No, not quite that! They would not have escaped from the dilemma 'join the Commonwealth or else' which had confronted them since the negotiations began, but they would almost certainly have extricated them-

selves from Downing Street and from London without signing
and without internal rupture. What would have happened
then is pure speculation. The Free State might not have been
set up so early, civil war would most probably have been
avoided. And partition would that have been with us today?

Those who do not know the story may wonder what exactly
it was that Griffith agreed to on November 12 and 13 beyond
his colleagues. The answer provided exhaustively in my book is
'Very little, if anything on paper'. But psychologically he was
made to feel a kind of commitment to the British which isolated
him from his colleagues at the crunch. This was enough to tip
the scale in favour of his announcement that he personally
would sign if no one else did. But never for a moment must we
forget that the kind of settlement being offered Ireland seemed
to him acceptable and honourable and probably everybody on
both sides of the table realized that this was his view. Nothing
but loyalty to his comrades had kept him from saying so and
that was cancelled in one of the greatest conflicts of duties we
can find in history when another loyalty—loyalty to his pledged
word—was thrown into the scale with the remorseless timing of
genius.

It is sometimes said that if only Mr. de Valera had been
leading the delegation in London, this nightmarish situation
could not have arisen. One day, it is to be hoped that the whole
working of his mind on this problem at the time and since will
be placed before the public even more fully than hitherto. The
fact remains as he has pointed out to me in conversation that
his staying at home was generally accepted in Ireland and the
question did not become a serious issue until the Articles of Agreement had been signed and the political division had occurred.

Nevertheless, he had decided at the Irish Cabinet meeting
on December 3 that it was his duty to go to London until
assured that the British proposals would not be signed in London
without reference back. Could he have foreseen the signature
that actually took place in the extraordinary circumstances of
December 5 and 6? I cannot think so—I shall never be able to
think so.

I said just now after indicating the limitations of the break on Ulster strategy that I had two further comments. One I have just made—a tactical criticism of its application; the other is more important, but the matter is so well known that I can be brief.

It was admitted from the British side by Lord Birkenhead, for example, that without the boundary clause the Treaty never would have been, never could have been signed. Certainly if it had not been for the expectations from the boundary commission which Michael Collins acquired from Lloyd George on the last morning he himself would never have agreed to sign and there would have been no Treaty. Wisely or foolishly the Irish believed that the boundary clause must bring them two counties or the equivalent and that the North would become a non-viable area as a result. But it was this very fact—that the North would become non-viable if the obvious interpretation of the clause were followed—which in fact led the Feetham Tribunal to decide four years later that this interpretation was impossible. By that time Lloyd George had long since disappeared from the government and as Professor Gilbert Murray said, 'it may so easily happen that one set of individuals give the promise and quite another act in breach of it'.

I simply cannot believe that anything like the Feetham decision which would have deprived the twenty-six counties of any real gain at all and was in the end washed out all round could have been given in 1922. In short, if I was asked to name one instance in recent years of Ireland collectively being let down by England collectively I would pick out the Boundary Commission. 'Ah well' an Englishman will say 'if the Irish hadn't made a civil war on each other, things couldn't have turned out that way.' To which an Irishman will reply—if it hadn't been for the ultimatum on December 5, there would have been no civil war. To which an Englishman—but enough is enough! The point I am concerned with now is that though the Irish strategy seemed to result in their getting neither of their objectives, neither the republic nor the unity of Ireland, they could legitimately feel on December 6 that they had gone a long way towards obtaining the latter, Irish Unity. Yet the seeming advantage escaped their clutches later.

So much for the question of Ulster. I said some while ago that while the theoretical agreement existed between the two main parties on the objective of unity there seemed then no way of softening the conflict on the constitutional issue about the future status of Ireland. By October, of course, both sides had moved a good way towards one another from what might be understood to be their positions in June. As late as June 21, 1921, the British Government were still insisting on the sub-ordinate parliament of the Act of 1920 and refusing autonomy to that subordinate parliament, even in its own internal finance. But on July 20 she had made an offer that purported to be one of dominion status—an offer that went much further than any previously made to Ireland. On her side Ireland had declared herself an Independent Republic in January 1919 and had been fighting for two years or more a guerrilla war under that banner. Yet by October in the draft treaty taken to London she agreed to become an external associate of the Commonwealth, with a status of course not less than the sovereign states of the Commonwealth. In later drafts it is explained that Ireland is to be associated with the British for matters of common concern which are to include defence, peace and war and, perhaps, political as distinct from commercial treaties. Irish citizens and citizens of the British Commonwealth would enjoy reciprocal rights, i.e. Irish citizens would enjoy the privileges of British citizenship and vice versa.

Gradually, to quote my own book, 'the Irish came to agree to recognize the Crown as Head in the foreign sphere where Ireland is to act in concert with the Commonwealth. But any arrangement which would involve allegiance (i.e. subordination in matters domestic, as well as in matters external, to the British monarch) or the presence of the King in the legislature (i.e. the Royal Veto) or common citizenship making Irishmen into British subjects, is resisted to the end.' Above all they could countenance no arrangement that made Ireland a British dominion. With its suggestion that Irishmen were 'Britain's children' by origin, enjoying their freedom only so long as Britain suffered them to do so. Nor could they contemplate the abandonment of the Republic, the symbol that their freedom was substantially complete. 'There was nothing theoretically impossible' I wrote in 1935, 'about a Republic not associated with but actually a member of the Empire, as a dominion. This arrangement was, however, not seriously put forward by either party, and throughout the choice lay between an externally associated Republic and a dominion within the Empire.' It was this choice, may I add now, that Mr. Lloyd George felt it his duty to insist upon at the point of the gun, on December 5, 1921. And though many people in England may have thought him too ruthless, there can be no doubt that British public opinion was for the most part behind him in insisting that dominion status was the furthest conceivable limit.

There has been such a liberalization of the Commonwealth since then; such a movement towards complete equality and liberty for all its members, that it is difficult to cast one's mind back sufficiently. When India in 1949 became a republic *inside* the Commonwealth, what was thought to be the unbridgeable gulf between the British and the Irish positions was leapt at a bound. But one must look back to 1921 when the members of the Commonwealth were still referred to as the dominions; when the phrase 'British Empire' was still used as often as 'British Commonwealth'; when the right of a member of the Commonwealth to secede had certainly not been established. One has to admit that Irish independence beyond the point already achieved by the middle of 1921 was probably impossible without further heavy sacrifices and further grave suffering.

But these are armchair speculations; they can never detract from the stature of the men concerned; the grandeurs and miseries of the chief Irish participants, Mr. de Valera, Arthur Griffith, Michael Collins Erskine Childers and the others were on an heroic scale. As the years have passed, as bitterness has diminished, as their country holds her head ever higher as a Christian community of international purpose, each of them takes his place, beyond argument or cavil, on the honoured roll of those who have lived and died for Ireland.

10

FROM THE TREATY TO THE CIVIL WAR

By Desmond Williams

THE CIVIL WAR of 1922 to 1923 is the great landmark in recent Irish history. If for the former ascendancy the Treaty marked the start of a new era, the civil war is the point of departure for most of the older people in this country. It is only in the last ten years or so that the Irish, especially the younger generation, have shown signs of approaching the story as history rather than personal politics. The civil war has often been held the mainspring of bitterness and cynicism in Irish social life. The creative talents flourishing before 1921 have often been contrasted with the apparent decline that followed. Some saw the war as an evil aberration. Yet it was preceded by a political revolution extending from the 1916 rising to the treaty. Civil wars have often broken out at the end of revolutionary periods. There was France, for example, between 1789 and 1799; the Republic of Weimar Germany; Soviet Russia; and now we have the Arabian states. Nothing is inevitable in these matters, but some things are more likely than others. Civil war commonly follows upon revolution conducted in the name of liberty. Such wars have a common pattern, when traditional modes of government are violently disrupted, or where sovereignty or jurisdiction are abandoned without effective replacements. The old order is gone; the new one waits to be shaped. Again in such wars the parties and persons involved think they have a monopoly of righteousness. Human

life has less value, for those engaged grow used to giving and
taking death as the fever proceeds. If war and victory have their
advantages, they have their drawbacks too. Youth holds sway
more obtrusively in such desperate times. Prudence and reflection are less prized than more flamboyant, martial virtues. And
civil feuds are more bitter, with more lasting consequences as
far as personal relationships are concerned. When friends fall
out, the daggers stay sharp. Families devour each other; the
nearer in blood the bloodier. The causes of civil, as of other
types of war, lie to some extent in the immediate past, and
responsibilities for action or the lack of it are seldom clear cut.
The participants rarely acknowledge this. But it cannot be
repeated too often that no one person or party is ever wholly to
blame for anything. Here again the Irish civil war was no
exception.

When did that war begin? And when did the old friends fall
out to the point of no return? To answer this query of date is in
part to answer other questions, such as why and how the
dispute arose. Wars in any but the formal sense do not usually
begin merely on the first day that shots are exchanged on both
sides; and even the side that fires the first shot may not be
primarily responsible.

But dates are important in tracing the chain of events that
lead to such decisive action. The conventional date for instance
for the start of our civil war is June 28, 1922, when the bombard-
ment of the Four Courts was initiated by forces under the
command of Michael Collins, as head of the provisional government, and Richard Mulcahy, as minister of defence of the
Government of Dáil Éireann. But occupation of the Courts of
Justice on April 14 was taken by many to be the real starting
point of the war. Others push the story further back to the
inauguration of raids in Tipperary and Cork under the
guerrilla leaders, Seamus Robinson and Sean Moylan, in
February, or to the holding of a prescribed Volunteer convention on March 26, in Dublin. And those who hold to this thesis
assert the existence months before June 28 of a virtual state of
war directed against the legitimate authorities set up January
10 by the people's representatives in the second Dáil. If you

supported the Free State, as it eventually came to be called, you then stressed events occurring long before June: if you were a Republican, opposed to Collins and Griffith, you tried to pin responsibility on happenings only weeks before the guns went off across the Liffey. So the participants differ even on the starting date. In fact, the origins have many starting dates. The true story is always organic, i.e. one in which all parties and their leaders are involved, and in which each displays in varying degrees consistency and inconsistency, courage or cowardice (physical or moral), steadiness or vacillation, foresight or recklessness, self or common interest. The lines crossed. Motives were often mixed, and from time to time the leaders seemed to change camps.

To take an example: Collins was the closest associate of Arthur Griffith, yet as head of the provisional government he not only admired de Valera on the other side but concluded with him the so-called Pact agreement on May 20, 1921—in the face of grave doubts expressed by Griffith and Kevin O'Higgins. Collins secured the respect of Churchill as a faithful party to the Treaty and he also signed agreements with Sir James Craig, head of the Northern Irish Government. Yet he partially violated these agreements shortly afterwards—and without the full knowledge of his ministerial colleagues in the provisional government or in the Dáil. In March 1921 he swapped arms with republican officers for use against the R.U.C. and organized a military campaign for mid-May against Orange strongposts throughout the six counties. This he did at a time when again Griffith, Cosgrave, O'Higgins and Blythe were passionately concerned to disarm the republicans in the south and maintain the articles of agreement with Britain. Of course, Collins had his reasons, but they were not reasons that the others would have accepted, if they had known them precisely. Such reasons were more intelligible to a former military colleague in the I.R.A. And I.R.B. such as Liam Lynch, the putative chief of staff of the republican forces, in mounting revolt against the Dáil from January to March.

The situation of de Valera was also obscure during those months though in another way. It was more what he said than

what he did that led to ambiguity regarding the ultimate
course he intended to take.

There was the celebrated speech of January 6 in which he
stated that as a labourer's child he knew his Irish people well
and that he only had to look into his own heart to know what
the Irish people wanted.

On January 5, he had published a proclamation in *An Phoblacht*,
which was construed by many as a warning of imminent
conflict:

> fellow-citizens! you are in danger; influences, more deadly
> to a nation faced by an enemy than a plague in its ranks, are at
> work among you ... stand fast, fellow citizens, by what you
> know to be right. Do not allow yourselves to be tempted from
> the straight and honourable path. If you quail at the conse-
> quences—what will they not ask you to surrender next to this
> ignoble fear?

There was also the much discussed utterance of March 16 in
which he referred to the possibility of people having to wade in
blood against those who had signed the treaty. There were two
interpretations one might well have placed on these words, one
long and the other short term, the former innocent from the
viewpoint of those primarily concerned to uphold law and order
at the time, the latter more pressing and far more dangerous.
De Valera may have known his position in abstract politics; but
others were far from sure what he was after at the time. His
heart, he made it clear, was with the young men, like Rory
O'Connor and Liam Mellows, who were out for action to defy
the Dáil, or harry the remaining British forces in Ireland (then
in the process of gradual evacuation under the terms of the
treaty). These youngsters, some still in their twenties, and
several under twenty, hoped to unify pro-treatyites and anti-
treatyites in a renewed war against the British. They hoped to
provoke the British to re-invade Ireland. The same idea was
entertained by the leading extremist on the other side, Henry
Wilson (who, by the way, had denounced the treaty as the
'liquidation of the empire'). Both O'Connor and Wilson were
all out to overthrow the middlemen.

If de Valera's heart was clear on this issue, where was his head? He did not lead the republican officers into war: they were trying to lead him into war, and the country in his tow. The former president's position appeared increasingly ambiguous. It might be said that the gravest charge opponents could cogently raise was not any action he took between the treaty and the civil war, but the leasing of his name to others. De Valera probably wanted reconciliation with Collins and Mulcahy. This he hoped to achieve by means of the Pact election, from which he thought a coalition government would emerge (with himself as minister of defence). Final decisions on the Treaty would be shelved and the old pre-Treaty front restored. His calculations went wrong. The Pact broke down. A 'republican' constitution was promised by Collins, with curious disregard for the actual terms of the Treaty. It was finally jettisoned—at the understandable insistence of the British Government, to whom it was eventually submitted. The republicans lost the election on June 16. The whole basis, therefore, of the pact, which had brought de Valera once again in touch with Collins, to the disapproval of Collins' ministerial partners, was destroyed.

A new chapter of conflict followed, this time within the camp of the Republican officers, including both those who had followed O'Connor and Mellows into the Four Courts on April 14 and those who still maintained touch with Collins—this latter connection being in part a by-product of former I.R.B. partnership. Some wanted immediate war. Others preferred to postpone it. O'Connor, Mellows, Barry and others—all very young men, by the way—wished to force the issue. Liam Lynch, along with Sean Moylan and his friends, still more or less under the continuing but distinct influence of de Valera and Collins were hoping to postpone the fighting and see how the new government shaped.

What were the motives of these young army men, who, as early as January 11, had protested against the treaty to Mulcahy as minister of defence and later denied any obligation of obedience to the Dáil or provisional government? Many doubtless were affected by what was said to be the paramount

I

obligation of the oath. But there were other reasons. These were young men, most of whom had fought during the Anglo-Irish war and now saw the creation of a new army at Beggar's Bush from the high posts of which they were excluded and which in certain cases were given to professional officers who had not actually fought in the Anglo-Irish war—or who had arrived late. A conflict over jobs. It is happening in Algeria today.

One of the leaders of this group gave fresh expression to typical sentiments on this matter in a speech in the Dáil on April 26:

> I am not quick on the draw, as I would like to be, but I am a gun-man. During the war the British called me the leader of the murder gang. And the minister by implication called me yesterday a leader of the robber gang. My men were ready to fight for the republic against England; they were promised that the army of the republic would be kept in being. These men are out of employment, without a smoke, badly-clad, and we are not all pussy-footers. We want, on occasion, a drink too. All that is the fault of the men who told us that the truce was a breathing stage. . . . During the war, my word went in north Cork. In any terms that could be applied to me today, my word goes yet. I robbed nineteen post-offices; in February last I issued an order in my area, seeing no other action taken by the Dáil to keep its promise to my men than that the dog-tax should be paid to me. The minister of defence has always been a good friend of mine, but I say to him that we unfortunate plain soldiers were easily gulled by the politicians here in the Dáil.

More will be said later about the split in republican ranks. At this point—from the election in mid-June—it must be mentioned that de Valera played no effective or observable role. To some extent he was a planet in a constantly changing constellation of forces and people, who were influenced either favourably or adversely more by his glamorous reputation than by his indecisive acts or speeches. After the shelling of the Four Courts by government forces on June 28, the republican forces divided since a convention meeting on June 18, now re-united in what they termed common defence against the 'Freestaters' using British cannons, by the way, loaned by the

British G.O.C. Macready. (What else could they use?) Now de Valera's position at this crucial moment is illustrated by the fact that he spent some part of June 28 drafting a peace proclamation, but a while later, preceded by Cathal Brugha (who had influenced him so much from August 1921), he joined the republican forces in action, and had himself enrolled as a simple soldier. He took no responsibility for the political actions of the army leaders. For he had not controlled them, nor had they sought his advice. Right up till the last, his position was unpredictable, maybe even to himself. As with Collins, the future was fluid. Both, one initially for the treaty, the other against it, had no straight path cut out for them.

This was not generally believed by de Valera's pro-treaty adversaries, whose information was warranted. The intelligence service run by Collins, which had worked so effectively against Dublin castle and the British occupying forces, withered rapidly away after December 6. Collins anyhow was now busily building up a new government, a legal system, an instrument of order in a new army and a police force designed for civil functions. At the same time he was involved in the higher spheres of diplomacy. He trotted over to London frequently to discuss the Constitution with the British, to arrange for the transfer of civil and military powers to a new Dublin castle and to establish some form of minimal co-opera-tion with Ulster and Craig. He was also doing his best to maintain links with former colleagues in the I.R.A. and I.R.B. His duties had multiplied; no longer was he simply director of intelligence, of G.H.Q., minister for finance and president of the I.R.B. He kept up all possible personal con-tacts: both with the republican wing under Liam Lynch and with officers commanding northern divisions of the I.R.A., who were not at all concerned with the problem of 'oath or no oath'. He tinkered constantly with the idea of recovering the lost sheep de Valera by promising a Janus-faced state accepting the treaty and yet parading a republican constitution. Bismarck was once said to have kept five balls in the air simultaneously. But Collins, who had also to work with his colleagues, few of whom completely agreed with his conciliatory efforts, was even more daring. He kept so many balls up his sleeves that he sometimes forgot the practical limits of political and human action.

Throughout all this Collins sometimes deceived not only himself but fellow ministers such as Griffith, Blythe, O'Higgins and Cosgrave, and the republican opposition. This lent dubious haze to the Dáil and provisional government policy. Collins remained dynamically boyish to the end, a genius of activism whose shrewd perception of people was mingled with naíve disregard for the customary processes of government.

De Valera and Collins, in their different ways, were responsible to a large extent, as it turned out, for the civil war. Collins tried to do too much, de Valera too little. Excess activity on one side seeming inertia on the other postponed a showdown that might well have occurred in February or April—and with success. The intentions were good but conduct in either case inappropriate.

The objective of most of his colleagues in the cabinet (whether of the Dáil or of the provisional government—an ambiguity arising out of necessity to combine the terms of the treaty with the republican concept of Dáil Éireann, as elected in 1918) was to set up a new state, based on law, and freedom within the bounds of the treaty. This involved the practical tasks of establishing a professional army, the re-introduction of an effective taxation system and the setting down of a new constitution, based in part on Irish tradition and even more on the legacy derived from the British parliamentary and legal system. For most of the cabinet the conflict over the treaty was settled by the Dáil's verdict on January 7. Collins and Mulcahy differed from their colleagues, not so much on the ultimate objective but on the method of obtaining it. They had fought with Lynch, Moylan, O'Connor (and de Valera) at one time or another; O'Higgins, Blythe and Griffith had never been military men. It was more difficult for Collins and Mulcahy to escape such links, especially when the republican leaders—or at least a section of them revolving around de Valera or Lynch—had not yet snapped them. So some efforts were made at the end of April to avert the spectre of violence.

The element of confusion referred to above did not arise out of the personal policies of the leaders of different groups. There were other important figures in the wings. The pro-treaty-forces also included the Church. Here the main concern, as usual, was peace. In general the non-political sections of the community favoured the treaty; but these forces were not represented in the Dáil of 1921. There the field lay wide open to the advanced nationalists. Griffith, Cosgrave, O'Higgins, etc. felt their responsibility covered the many citizens unaffected by republicanism: the southern unionists, for instance the trade unionists, as well as those who seldom bothered about politics.

The difficulties of effective government were increased, if not originated by confusion over jurisdiction, sovereignty and power. In the early months of 1922, there were, in fact, at least four groups competing for sovereign power in parts of all of the country. In the south there were three groups: the Government of the Dáil, first set up in 1919 under Griffith, deriving its authority from the Dáil; the provisional government under Collins, which worked with Griffith and was the only authority recognized by the British; and the army executive under O'Connor and Lynch. The army executive did not recognize the Dáil or the provisional government. De Valera, as leader of the constitutional wing of the republican movement recognized the Dáil, but not the provisional government. Collins and Griffith recognized both the Dáil and the provisional government, the latter only theoretically, as subordinate to the former. In fact, Dáil Éireann was nothing more than a showpiece which served as a useful stage for preserving the trappings of republicanism.

As Shakespeare once said in Macbeth: 'Confusion now hath made its masterpiece!'

If confusion abounded in practice, each side was careful to observe the purity of its logic—depending on the initial axiom: There were those, perhaps many outside the elected circle of 1918, who failed to rise to these levels of sophistication, or, if they did, became tired of it. But for others the theology of the dispute was all-important—especially when it related to ulti-mate power in the state, or to the personalities who would inherit that power.

Policy became suffused with personality. Words uttered in temper finalised fronts and possibly distorted the course of events. Griffith rejected the right of Erskine Childers 'as a damned Englishman' to speak and be heard in the Dáil. In a journal set up by O'Higgins and others, he was pursued as a former British intelligence agent and as a man suffering from mental rather than moral disorder. In another pro-treaty newspaper, de Valera was attacked as not having the instincts of an Irishman. Collins had been sneered at as one of the 'incompetent amateurs who had seized the helm of the ship of the Irish state and had driven it on to the rocks'. On March 12, he retaliated by referring to 'the captain who was away from his ship'—that time in America—'when the weather was very stormy'. On the anti-treaty side, Collins was a butt for republican wits as a Fleet Street hero who had invented a reputation for himself by handing out exaggerated accounts of his war enterprises to the British and American press. Miss Mac Sweeney, one of the republican ladies, accused Mulcahy of a 'most abominable piece of felon-setting', and Collins of 'doing for Ireland what Castlereagh had done'. The republican ladies were quite conspicuous for dramatic interventions of this kind.

Even Cathal Brugha referring to the I.R.B. in the Dáil said 'there is only one way that the dastards responsible for disestablishing the republic can ever extirpate this crime. And it is by dying for Ireland'. This was on May 19, the very day before Collins and de Valera concluded their pact for the election of the next Dáil. Brugha had been *le brave des braves* —perhaps the most singly heroic of those who had fought with Collins against the English.

Meanwhile Collins asserted the jurisdiction of the republican army in the north—provoked by the Orange pogroms in Belfast, which mounted as from March. (A Catholic family, man, woman and children, were slaughtered that month.) In Ulster there were the I.R.A., the newly formed R.U.C., and the British army—a less confused situation than in the south, since the R.U.C. and the British army worked together. Republic and treaty, however, meant more to the southerners in these months than partition.

But developments in Ulster in May and early June temporarily strengthened the ties between Collins and the republican soldiers under Lynch. Through the Beggars' Bush barracks, though not through Merrion Street, Collins had collaborated indirectly with republican forces in border actions against the R.U.C. in February and March. In the unsuccessful campaign of May, and in renewed futile conflicts around Belleek and Pettigo in early June, Collins or his agents were again involved. Then it all faded away. The northern I.R.A. kept largely apart from southern controversies throughout; a number of their leaders, Frank Aiken for example, opposed the holding of a republican convention in March 1922 and stayed neutral until the civil war covered the twenty-six counties. These episodes are, perhaps, the sorriest part of the story.

Another principal party remained—the British Government. The British backed the provisional government all along, putting up patiently enough with what some of them judged as provocation, tergiversation and vacillation on the part of the pro-treatyites. But it was British intervention after the assassination of Sir Henry Wilson on June 22 that, along with Four Courts kidnapping and raiding incidents, induced Collins to wipe out the O'Connor–Barry centre of opposition still sitting there in the Four Courts. O'Connor etc., for their part, were about to launch an attack on the remnants of the British army, in Dublin. Between British pressures resulting from the killing of Wilson and pressures bred in the Four Courts, Collins (with Mulcahy more hesitant) at last took the decision, urged on him for months by Griffith and O'Higgins, to clear out the occupants of the Four Courts. This was not in response to a British ultimatum though it probably anticipated one. In fact General Macready had on the previous day dissuaded Lloyd George and the secretary of war, Churchill, from going about the same business. In Macready's view, 'if it had to be done, it were better done by the Irish'. The Republicans, divided so far, came together and the war began.

All wars are the product of indecision, chance, misunderstanding, and personal will. They come from the environment in which people work and the conviction of those in power. The war under discussion might have started earlier, or later. In either case, the outcome for Ireland would have been different. Perhaps the extremists on both sides alone knew their own minds and the contingent situation better than those of more moderate opinions. But moderation, reluctance to engage in a war with one's own countrymen may be of greater value than the confidence and arrogance of those who see right and wrong too clearly. The balance between the forces of liberty and order may have depended upon those who found it hardest to decide between black and white, even if muddle and panic deriving from these decisions greatly contributed to the origins and conduct of this particular war. A full state of war lasted for nearly a year, but its after effects for much longer.

I I

IRELAND AND THE BRITISH COMMONWEALTH OF NATIONS: THE DOMINION SETTLEMENT

By Nicholas Mansergh

L OST CAUSES seem to be my lot! In the Thomas Davis lectures on *The Shaping of Modern Ireland* my theme was John Redmond and The Third Home Rule Bill; tonight it is Irish membership of the British Commonwealth, a cause not only lost—well lost many may think—but also, in the context of the dramatic events of forty years ago, dull. Yet at the time Ireland's status as a dominion within the Commonwealth aroused emotions, the intensity of which succeeding generations find it increasingly hard to comprehend. And surely contemporaries were right to feel so strongly. Dominion status was the substance of the settlement; the purpose and the life-force without which the Treaty was meaningless. Dull it may be; indispensable to understanding it none the less remains.

The factual record is concise and clear. Ireland became a dominion on December 6, 1921. The first article of the Treaty stated that she should have the same constitutional status in the community of nations known as the British Empire as the Dominion of Canada, the Commonwealth of Australia, the Dominion of New Zealand and the Union of South Africa. The second and the third articles of the Treaty defined the Irish position more closely by saying that her relation to the Imperial Parliament and Government should be that of the Dominion of Canada and that the Governor-General should be appointed in like manner as Canadian Governor-General. The fourth article prescribing the terms of the Oath, which Lord Birkenhead regrettably enough may *not* have described as 'the greatest piece of prevarication in history', made particular reference to Irish membership of the group of nations forming the British Commonwealth of Nations. In sum these provisions left no room for doubt about the fact that the Irish Free State was to be a dominion. But they invited two larger questions—why dominion status for Ireland? And what was a dominion? Let me try to offer some answer to each in turn.

Why dominion status for Ireland? There is a simple answer. It was imposed by the British. It was accepted by the Irish plenipotentiaries following upon an ultimatum—the word is Churchill's—and on pain of a resumption of immediate and terrible war—the phrase is President de Valera's. But is it a sufficient answer? Hardly. In so far as it implies that dominion status was altogether objectionable to the Irish and altogether acceptable to the British it is misleading. It was neither.

The problem central to the whole negotiations was indicated in Lloyd George's question—how might the association of Ireland with the community of nations known as the British Empire best be reconciled with Irish national aspirations? The answer, in the Irish view, was not by dominion status. On this, so far as I know, the Dáil cabinet were unanimous in the summer of 1921. Their demand was for a republic, in some way externally associated, if need be, with the British Commonwealth. And it was with suggestions to this end that they sought to counter British proposals for dominion status. In respect of form the two ideas were incompatible. Republican status was inconsistent with dominion status. In one sense this was all-important. Mr. Lloyd George and President de Valera, however much they might differ on lesser matters, agreed on what was fundamental. To both men it was the symbols of sovereignty that signified most. But there, of course, their agreement ended; Lloyd George never failing in his insistence that the monarchical symbolism of the crown must be the essential feature of the settlement and de Valera resolved that the republic should not be sacrificed. In this conflict the British view prevailed, was imposed if you like, with dominion status. It was the Crown, not the republic, that was embodied in the Treaty and later, in a form as diluted as its draftsmen could devise, in the constitution of the Irish Free State. This presence of the Crown in the constitution, was a distinguishing feature, common to all dominions, of dominion status. Whether on the broader view it was the most important feature was a matter on which men were, and no doubt long will be, deeply divided.

There was, in any case, more to dominion status than the symbolism of monarchy. There was an expanding, if still debatable, area of freedom. The dominions, Canada, Australia, New Zealand and South Africa, which had entered the First World War as British colonies, ended as separate signatories to the Peace Treaties at Versailles. They were foundation members of the new international organization, the League of Nations. They had long been wholly self-governing in their domestic affairs and by 1921 two among them at least, Canada and South Africa, were seeking to secure for themselves corresponding independence in international affairs, so that they might for example assume international obligations, or not assume them, as their own parliaments and governments saw fit, enter treaties or not enter into them as their own governments decided and generally be in no way obliged to follow British foreign policies. True, the growing practice of equality was still counterbalanced by the theory of subordination. But might not this by a concerted effort and with Irish reinforcement soon be altogether removed? True also, there was the fear, strongly voiced by President de Valera and by Erskine Childers that in the case of Ireland geographical propinquity would mean a diminution of dominion powers. But would the overseas dominions acquiesce in any such curtailment? In sum was there not at least a prospect that in terms of independence Irish national aspirations might be reconciled with membership of the community of nations known as the British Commonwealth through dominion status? Did it not in its own way provide much of the substance of what Sinn Féin had been fighting for? Were there not assets in respect of power to offset liabilities in respect of constitutional forms? At any rate, in whatever way the balance of argument and probability was deemed to fall, here was something different in kind from Home Rule.

If dominion status was not without advantages for the Irish; it was assuredly not without objection for the British. And moreover what was especially attractive about it on the Irish side, namely the prospect of expanding freedom, was precisely what was objectionable about it to many on the British side. If Lloyd George's approach to dominion status for Ireland was unusually devious, there was at least a reason for it. He was the Liberal leader of a coalition cabinet dependent on the support of a great Unionist majority for survival in office. This majority may not have been made up, as was said after the 1918 election, of a lot of hard-faced men who looked as if they had done well out of the war but at any rate it was made up of men for the most part hostile, and in some few cases almost pathologically hostile, to the idea of a self-governing Ireland. They talked about Lloyd George as 'the great little man who had won the war' but in matters on which emotion ran high he was not a free agent. He was the prisoner of the coalition, a prisoner who more than once, so we are told, thought of escape by resignation. It was not he, but his defeated and much abused predecessor Asquith who, in 1919, first formally proposed dominion status for Ireland. The proposal was received by Unionists with howls of execration. And why? Bonar Law, the Canadian Unionist leader in the coalition, well remembered for his pre-war assault on Home Rule, gave one telling reason. The connection of the dominions with the Empire, he warned the House of Commons in 1920, depended upon themselves. If 'they choose tomorrow', he said, 'to say "we will no longer make a part of the British Empire" we would not try to force them'. Dominion status for Ireland, therefore, might mean first secession, then an independent republic. The very idea of dominion status must accordingly be resisted root and branch. Lloyd George gave every appearance of doing so. Further dominion status proposals from Asquith elicited from him the comment 'was ever such lunacy proposed by anybody?' That was October 1920. In July 1921 he was warmly commending a dominion status settlement to Mr. de Valera. This time the suggestion had not come, immediately at least, from a British but from a Commonwealth source.

On June 13, 1921 General Smuts, then prime minister of South Africa, lunched with King George V at Windsor Castle. He found the King anxiously preoccupied about the speech he was shortly to deliver at the opening of the Northern Ireland Parliament. The draft submitted to the King by the Irish Office was reputedly 'a blood thirsty document'. General Smuts suggested something altogether different. He prepared a draft which he sent with a letter to Lloyd George. In it, Smuts spoke of the Irish situation as 'an unmeasured calamity' and 'a negation of all the principles of government' for which the Commonwealth stood. He suggested that the King's speech in Belfast should contain a promise of dominion status for Ireland, a promise which he felt sure, would have the support of all the dominion prime ministers. Lloyd George did not agree and the promise was not made. But the idea of dominion status was given new point and urgency.

On July 4 dominion status was formally put forward by the British Government as a basis of settlement. True the offer was so hedged about with reservations subtracting from it, that Lloyd George was left open to Mr. de Valera's retort that the principle of the proposed pact was not easy to determine. But none the less, from the British point of view, the offer was decisive. It was one to which the majority of the coalition's supporters were instinctively opposed. Their hearts were with the prime minister when he denounced dominion status as insanity; against him when he recommended it as a basis of settlement. Yet in England there was one thing greatly in its favour.

Dominion status was an experiment which had been tried elsewhere and had succeeded. The union of English and French in the Dominion of Canada was thought of as a major triumph of English statesmanship, while fresh in the minds of Lloyd

George, Chamberlain and Churchill was the success of the policy of trust and reconciliation which brought into being the Union of South Africa. Austen Chamberlain, at the time leader of the Unionist party and son of Joseph Chamberlain, the man who had killed the first Home Rule Bill, said explicitly that it was the success of those Liberal policies in South Africa, which brought a South African dominion into existence, that more than anything else persuaded him to break with his own cherished convictions and his party's tradition and sponsor a dominion settlement of the Irish question. In England it is much easier to take a revolutionary step if you can say 'we have travelled this road before'. But in Ireland the advance was to be by untrodden ways.

That might not have mattered quite so much but for one thing. Dominion status lacked precision. It was conceived of, not as something possessing final form at any given point in time, but as something in process of continuing development. In negotiation this was an undoubted liability. Uncertainties implicit in the status served greatly to accentuate mistrust and suspicion, the British coming to regard President de Valera as 'a visionary' likely to see mountains where they saw only molehills, while the Irish thought of Lloyd George as a master of political dexterity, not to say duplicity, who used the liberal imperial vocabulary of Gladstone to further the purposes of Castlereagh. Yet the problem at root was more than personal. Even at this distance in time it is not easy to say concisely and with precision—and here I come to my second question—what dominion status for Ireland did involve.

In the House of Commons debate on the Treaty, Lloyd George asked himself the self-same question. What, he said, does dominion status mean? But he did not answer it. He talked instead, and not unreasonably, of the dangers of definition, of limiting development by too many finalities, of introducing rigidities alien to British constitutional thinking. He was prepared to say what dominion status did not mean. But not what it did. The Treaty, as we have seen, defined dominion status by analogy, that is, by saying that the status of the Irish Free State would be that of the other dominions which it listed by name and more particularly that of Canada. The British prime minister was prepared to go no further. But we can perhaps do so, without plunging into constitutional detail, by looking at dominion status through the eyes of the dominions.

In 1921 the dominions conveniently enough were debating their own status. General Smuts was foremost among those who wished to have dominion status more clearly defined. Smuts repudiated Empire; he championed Commonwealth. The dominions, he pointed out, enjoyed a large measure of equality in practice but in law and constitutional form they were subordinate to the United Kingdom. He wanted the theory brought into line with practice. In a memorandum, circulated to the British Cabinet but not published till many years later, Smuts warned that unless this course were followed the Commonwealth would be faced with other Irelands, with other examples of doing too little and being too late. At the Imperial Conference in London, in June 1921, the issue was joined. Smuts was opposed notably by Australia's prime minister, W. M. Hughes. Hughes did not like the idea of defining imperial relations. There was no need for it. 'The difference between the status of the dominions now and twenty-five years ago' he said, 'is very great. We were colonies, we became dominions. We have been accorded the status of nations. . . . . What greater advance is conceivable? What remains to us? We are like so many Alexanders. What other worlds have we to conquer?' Neither the South Africans, nor the Canadians were persuaded. There were other worlds they wished to conquer. But at that crucial moment in the summer of 1921 it was hard, if only because of this still unresolved debate, for Lloyd George, or for the Irish, or for anyone else, to forecast with certainty how dominion relations would develop—how hard you can imagine by asking yourself tonight what relations between the countries of the Common Market will be in twenty or thirty years time.

We know now the tide of dominion nationalism was flowing too strongly to be checked. 'The fact of Canadian and South African independence' said Michael Collins in the Treaty debate 'is something real and solid and will grow in reality and force as time goes on.' That certainly proved to be true. He was right, too, in saying, 'We have got rid of the word Empire', and that in its place there was the British Commonwealth of Nations—the term itself with its very different overtones making its first official appearance in Article IV of the Treaty. Kevin O'Higgins who, like most supporters of the Treaty, did not believe that dominion status was the fulfilment of Ireland's destiny, hoped none the less that what remained would be won by agreement and by peaceful political evolution. That, too, proved substantially true. Dominion status despite the fears of some of its critics and, perhaps even more important, despite the forms with which it was still enshrouded, conferred a substantial measure of freedom and opened the way for complete independence. I think this might have been more generally recognized at the time, but for one thing. Kevin O'Higgins, to my mind, put his finger on it when he said that the most objectionable aspect of the Treaty was the threat of force that had been used to influence Ireland to a decision to enter what he called 'this miniature League of Nations'. He went on 'It has been called a League of Free Nations. I admit in practice it is so; but it is unwise and unstatesmanlike to bind any such League by any ties other than purely voluntary ties . . . I quite admit that in the case of Ireland the tie is not voluntary . . . the status is not equal.' Ireland was forced into a free association. That contradiction, that handicap, laid upon dominion status when Lloyd George foreclosed debate on December 5, 1921, with an ultimatum, clung to it like an old man of the sea, shaken off only when dominion status itself was discarded.

Many particular objections to dominion status were, of course raised in the Treaty Debate—objections about the subordination that it might mean in respect of the Crown or its representative, the Governor-General, or the armed forces or the judiciary. But in fact such limitations upon Irish, or for that matter upon dominion sovereignty, did not very long survive. At the first Imperial Conference at which the Irish played an active part, in 1926, the process of re-defining Commonwealth relations was begun. Lord Balfour, familiar forty years earlier as 'Bloody Balfour', presided in his old age 'with a smile like moonlight on a tombstone', according to Kevin O'Higgins, over the deliberations of a committee which opened the way for the last stage in the advance of the dominions to the unquestioned independence they have enjoyed since the Second World War. In 1931, with the enactment of the statute of Westminster, what remained of the old colonial Empire had been pulled asunder and Mr. Patrick McGilligan had reason for claiming in the Dáil that the Irish had played a large part in doing it. In that sense dominion status gave freedom to achieve freedom. It may not have been the goal but it had opened the way to the goal. The road to it was, however, slow and winding and in time of great transition young men generally prefer to travel by faster ways.

But if, as the historian must, one probes a little further one finds oneself looking again at the problem central to the debate in 1921 in another light. How might the association of Ireland with the community of nations known as the British Empire best be reconciled with Irish national aspirations? Canadians and Australians had advanced with satisfaction from colonial to dominion status. This was a road along which they wished to travel. They felt it was a road along which it was natural they should travel. They were countries of settlement. In Ireland there were counties of settlement—in the north-east. In a dominion their inclusion was the natural, their exclusion the illogical thing. For the rest, Ireland was not a country of settlement. It was one of the historic nations of Europe. It was not extra-European but European national symbolism to which it aspired. The Republic, not dominion status, was the goal. The point was put with characteristic forthrightness by Austin Stack in the Treaty debate. 'Let us assume,' he said, 'that under the Treaty Ireland will enjoy full Canadian powers. But,' he went on, 'I for one cannot accept from England full Canadian powers, three-quarter Canadian powers, or half Canadian powers. I stand for what is Ireland's right, full independence and nothing short of it.' What was natural and appropriate for the existing dominions would be in effect unnatural and inappropriate, at any rate, for a partitioned Ireland. The countries that were dominions in 1921 might seek independ-

K

ence, but Ireland was seeking something more as well—
independence and recognition of a separate national identity.
Dominion status at that time might lead to the one without
necessarily including the other. And to that extent dominion
status was conceived, and well conceived, but for another
situation. And in so far as the British believed that by conceding
dominion status to Ireland, she would become a dominion psychologically as well as constitutionally they were mistaken.

And here I come back to a simple but basic fact: dominion
status in 1921 was not compatible with republican status.
Allegiance to the Crown was then an essential feature of it.
That allegiance had to be expressed in the form of an oath.
That oath was embodied in the Treaty; it was embodied in the
constitution and it could not be removed (because of the
fundamental status given to the provisions of the Treaty by
the Constitution Act) without denouncing the Treaty and
dominion status of which the oath, at British insistence, was an
integral part. It was because this was so that Mr. de Valera
said in the Treaty debate: 'I am against the Treaty because it
does not do the fundamental thing.' It did not recognize, as
he claimed external association would have done, the separate,
distinct existence of a Republic. On the contrary, it gave away
Republican independence by bringing Ireland as a dominion
within the British Empire and more precisely, as he said, by
according recognition to the King as the source of executive
authority in Ireland. Over against, therefore, the substance (in
part still prospective) of freedom there had to be placed the
abandonment of the symbolism which expressed national
aspirations. The distinction between dominion status and external association was sharp rather than broad and that helps
to explain why the division that ensued was deep and lasting.
There are times when constitutional forms express things that
for many men matter most and this was one of them.

It was because this was so that the debate on dominion
status in Ireland—it sounds paradoxical but I am sure it is
true—enlarged the experience of the British Commonwealth
of Nations and will always hold its interest far beyond the
bounds of these islands. The question posed in 1921 might be

rephrased to read: how may national, republican aspirations best be reconciled with a monarchical, imperial or Commonwealth states system? The suggested answer on the Irish side was External Association, something that would possess the substance of dominion status but replace its monarchical with republican forms. In 1921 that solution was deemed impossible of consideration, as politically it then was, by the British negotiators. India, a historic nation of another continent, later posed the same problem, coupled with an explicit wish to remain a member-state of the Commonwealth as a republic. The Indians were fully familiar with the Irish background as I myself can testify, having discussed these matters in Delhi in 1946 with the members of a committee concerned with the drafting of the Indian republican constitution. Profiting by Irish experience, the problem of republican India's relations with the Commonwealth was resolved in 1949; the formula by which India acknowledged the King as Head of the Commonwealth being virtually identical with the formula proposed by President de Valera for the same purpose in Document No. 2 in 1922. The Commonwealth henceforward has had complete constitutional, as well as political, equality, its member states being monarchical or republican as they themselves desire. But by the time the British found the answer, the Irish had lost interest in the question.

12

THE IRISH QUESTION IN BRITISH POLITICS

(1916–1922)

By C. L. Mowat

'IRELAND, IRELAND! that cloud in the west, that coming
storm.' So Gladstone in 1845, so British politicians and the
British public in the period from 1916 to 1922. The Irish
question had been, of course, a familiar feature in the British
scene for centuries, a volcano, unpredictable, exasperating,
erupting from time to time, often with more smoke than fire.
Now in these years it produced its last and most violent eruption
and then subsided, spent, hardly smouldering. Nothing in the
history of the Irish question is so surprising as the suddenness
and completeness of its end. It simply disappeared as a major
factor in British politics.

In 1914 the position was relatively simple. The Liberals and
the Irish Nationalist Party wanted Home Rule for Ireland, the
Conservatives bitterly and militantly opposed it. It would be
untrue to say that the Irish question alone divided the Conservatives and Liberals; but beside it the other issues of the day
were all small potatoes. The Irish question overcame all else
with a fury which is now hard to believe or to understand.
Indeed, the Conservatives called themselves the Unionist Party,
as if the preservation of the Union alone mattered in British
politics.

The outbreak of the war with Germany put the Irish question

141

.aside. True, the Home Rule Bill was enacted, to the indignation of the Conservatives, but its operation was suspended. Next May, in 1915, Asquith formed a coalition government, bringing together Liberals and Conservatives, and including Carson as Attorney-General. The inclusion of the Ulster Unionist leader in the government was a blow to Redmond and the Nationalists—almost a slap in the face. To their growing isolation from the Irish public was now added their isolation within parliament, and the heart went out of the party.

The Easter rising of 1916 brought the Irish question again before parliament and public in Britain. Its character was misunderstood, partly because the news of it, at first censored by the government, appeared in driblets; it was not until Thursday April 27, three days after the rising, that *The Times*, for example, published a full report of the events in Dublin. It would doubtless have been galling to see it as a national uprising; in fact *The Times*' first report (on Tuesday 25) was of 'A raid on Ireland. German attempt to land arms.' Concentration on the German element, and on the unpreparedness of the Irish Government under Birrell's long administration, drew attention away from the national and revolutionary spirit of the revolt. Not until May 1, when it published the text of the Proclamation of the Provisional Government of the Republic of Ireland, would *The Times* reader have much idea what the rising was about.

It is not surprising, therefore, that the government reacted with a blind hitting back, a policy of terror after the rebellion had been quelled. It was not only the Unionist-Conservative members who demanded this: in a debate in the House of Lords on May 10 to 11 the chief critic of the government was a Liberal, Lord Loreburn, who was supported by Lord Midleton and other Irish peers and by Conservatives like Lords Halsbury, Salisbury and Cromer. Martial law was proclaimed, and General Maxwell carried out the summary trials and executions of thirteen of the leaders. The policy of sternness had plenty of support. *The Times* declared: 'nothing can be more cruel or more unwise in insurrections than half-hearted measures of suppression. They encourage fresh dupes to join the rebels, and

so increase the ultimate number of victims.' At the same time
it described a large number of prisoners who were embarked
at North Wall for Holyhead on April 30 as of two types: the
rabble class, and the 'intellectual', described as 'a young man
with a high forehead and thin firmly set lips'. The *Spectator*,
rebutting the *Manchester Guardian's* condemnation of the executions, that they were 'becoming an atrocity', wrote 'an atrocity
to execute a very few of the leaders of a rising deliberately
designed to make the Germans our masters—a rising which
murderously took the lives of hundreds of soldiers and
civilians. . . . !'

Yet there was opinion on the other side, which helped bring
the government back to a more moderate policy. The independent Liberal weekly, the *Nation*, under H. W. Massingham's
great editorship, was notably well informed about the rising.
Very early it recorded its 'deep concern' at the court martials
and the haste of the procedure: it had expected more deliberate
and merciful dealing. The government had thrown away a
great opportunity of killing 'this *opéra bouffe* revolt' by ridicule.
Let Carson and Redmond, it added, make a treaty of peace
under which Home Rule could become operative. 'The Irish
situation still lies in the hands of these two men. A few months
more and it will be beyond them.' A grim prophecy. A fortnight
later (May 20) Massingham, writing from Dublin, told his
readers how this 'obscure and abortive rising' had won the
sympathy of those who at the time had fiercely condemned it:
'it is the executions and the errors of the military administration . . . which have changed the mind of Irish Nationalism on
the perspective and the historical significance of the revolt.' A
priest had told him that for one sympathizer with Sinn Féin
on Easter Monday there were ten today.

In this belated work of education the Irish Nationalists in
parliament took a large part. A dozen or more of them asked
questions, day by day, about persons arrested, about executions,
about military expeditions into peaceful districts, above all
about the shooting of Sheehy-Skeffington. It was an English
Liberal member, R. D. Holt, on May 9, who drew the government's attention to the grave concern of many people in

England about the military executions. It was Dillon, on May
11, who told the full story of Sheehy-Skeffington's murder, who
pointed out how General Maxwell's rule was maddening the
people and spreading insurrection. He was proud of the rebels,
but it was the first rebellion in which the Irish majority had
been on the English side, 'and now you are washing out our
whole life work in a sea of blood'. Ireland might well be
grateful that she had such men at Westminster then, though
she has given them small thanks.

For they helped to turn the government. Asquith reasserted
his leadership and himself went to Ireland; the executions
ceased. Too late, of course; they had done their work. And, as
if to emphasize the futility of British policy, Asquith's next
move, on his return from Ireland, a new attempt to put Home
Rule into operation, was ruined by his Conservative-Unionist
colleagues.

Lloyd George negotiated, at the government's request, with
Redmond and Carson in June 1916. He got the consent of both,
and they in turn of the Ulster Nationalists and Unionists, to
Home Rule with the exclusion of Ulster for the duration of the
war. There were difficulties over the formula for this—and
Lloyd George may well have over-reached himself in his
assurances to both sides. None the less it was the Conservatives
within the government, principally Lord Lansdowne, Walter
Long and Lord Selborne (who himself resigned), who brought
the proposal to naught by insisting that the exclusion of Ulster
must be stated to be permanent. The same thing happened in
1917, when a Cabinet committee drafted another Home Rule
Bill, which Addison and other Liberals believed should be
enacted even without Nationalist support: they thought Ireland
would accept a *fait accompli* (including a partial separation of
Ulster). Redmond rejected the proposal, but it was also
Conservative opposition, particularly from Long and Bonar
Law, that led to its abandonment in favour of the abortive
Irish Convention. Finally there was a long struggle in April to
June 1918, when Lloyd George again moved for immediate
Home Rule as a counterpart to the application of conscription
to Ireland. Meetings of Unionist and Conservative M.P.s,

deputations, furious speeches and articles caused the government to back down.

At the end of the war the position was both the same and different. The same because the government was still a coalition, led by Lloyd George and Bonar Law. This meant that there was no dangerous Opposition Party in parliament but this did not eliminate opposition over Irish policy; rather, it meant that the Conservatives, as the majority party in the coalition, could veto any Irish measure which they disliked. The difference was that the Irish Nationalist Party virtually disappeared in the general election of December 1918 and that the successful Sinn Féin candidates, constituting themselves the Dáil Éireann, declared war on Great Britain.

British policy towards Ireland during the next two tormented years, 1919 to 1921, consisted of three parts. The first was legislative, a new Home Rule Bill, sluggishly debated and enacted in 1920. Ireland was to be given Home Rule at last—too late—but the price was partition, which the Conservatives demanded and the Ulster Unionists grudgingly accepted, retreating into their six-county enclave. The intention of the bill, however, was to preserve some unity in Ireland by means of an all-Ireland Council: the pious hope was expressed that partition would be merely temporary. This bill was passed, it should be noticed, by a House of Commons in which southern Ireland was virtually unrepresented.

The second policy was war: to put down insurrection and murder by the counter-measures of raids, arrests, reprisals by the Black-and-Tans and the army; or, to put it another way, to restore order and enforce the new Home Rule Act. The policy was doomed from the start: you cannot set bounds to the march of a nation. We have seen this tragic tale enacted by British governments again and again since, in Palestine, Ghana, Cyprus; and it threatens once again in Rhodesia. Strong words, the strong arm, arrests, repression, the uncompromising refusal to negotiate or to concede anything until order is restored and surrender made; then, when blood has been shed, good will dissipated, and the bitter resolution of the people has been confirmed, the British public has sickened of the policy carried

out in its name, the tough words have been eaten, the withdrawal negotiated. It was Ireland's tragedy to be the first to
endure this weary cycle, Britain's to learn nothing from it. A
tale familiar to us was new forty years ago. Until then Britain
had been able to enforce and restore law in colonial countries,
following this by a magnanimous concession of self-government;
at least this had happened in South Africa, and the earlier
failure of this policy towards the American colonies had been
forgotten.

The policy of war was, then, inevitable. British and Irish
might be sick of trench warfare; but the Great War had
engendered violence, and many in both countries were ready
to use it. Any government will react to assassination and arson
with strong measures: Lloyd George, head of a victorious
coalition but with Conservatives and Unionists predominating
in his majority, could hardly do otherwise. And his Chief of the
Imperial General Staff, Sir Henry Wilson, urged him on. And
yet from the very start of the strong-arm policy, in April 1920,
a third policy, that of negotiation, of making contact with the
Sinn Féin leaders and seeking for a truce and a settlement, was
being followed. Sir John Wheeler-Bennett's recent life of Sir
John Anderson reminds us how the new team at Dublin Castle,
particularly Anderson and 'Andy' Cope, pursued the two
courses simultaneously, under orders from London: Anderson
and Arthur Griffith met as early as September 26, 1920. The
grisly farce of shootings and raids, ambushes and reprisals, was
merely a cover for negotiations to concede, apparently to force,
in 1921 what had been refused to reason in 1920. Or was it?
Would Ireland have accepted the Free State, at the price of
partition, and Britain have accepted separation, with the
solatium of the six counties, without traversing first the way of
blood and shame?

In parliament the policy of force was attacked from the
beginning. Asquith and the independent Liberals, and Labour
members, were constant in their questions, and Sir Hamar
Greenwood was made more and more uncomfortable as the
sorry tale of shootings by members of the Crown forces, and
'unofficial' reprisals, was revealed. Asquith called the death of

Mrs. Quinn from shots fired by police 'a case of wilful murder'. The Labour Party asked for an inquiry into affairs in Ireland: when this was refused it appointed its own commission under Arthur Henderson, sent it to Ireland, and published its comprehensive and damning report. It followed this by a national campaign for peace and the election of a constitutional assembly in Ireland in January and February 1921. Large meetings were held in Free Trade Hall, Manchester and in the Albert Hall in London, and smaller meetings, attended by between 500 and 5,000 people, all over the country—in all 500 meetings within a month. Two editions of the Labour Commission's Report (20,000 copies) were sold, and 7,000,000 leaflets about Ireland were distributed. Nor were all Conservatives silent. Lord Robert Cecil proposed a commission of inquiry; Lord Henry Cavendish-Bentinck crossed the floor on the Irish issue; the Archbishop of Canterbury condemned reprisals in a speech in the Lords: 'you cannot cast out devils by calling in other devils.'

The upsurge of public feeling against the government's policy was remarkable and compelling. The incidents of the Black-and-Tan war were fully reported in the British press, and at least one reporter, Hugh Martin of the *Daily News*, was threatened with violence by the Black-and-Tans in Tralee for his unguarded reports of their reprisals. Liberal newspapers like the *Daily News*, the *Manchester Guardian* and the *Westminster Gazette* were opposed to Lloyd George and to the policies of his government on political grounds. So was *The Times*, partly because of Lord Northcliffe's feud against Lloyd George but also, more constructively, because of the enlightened views of a great editor, Wickham Steed. In addition books describing the state of affairs in Ireland were published very quickly, notably Hugh Martin's *Ireland in Insurrection* in 1921 and the anonymous *Administration of Ireland, 1920*, also published in 1921 (its author, 'I. O.', was C. J. C. Street).

As early as June 1919 *The Times* engaged a young Irish barrister, R. J. H. Shaw, as its Irish adviser. Shaw wrote ten articles entitled 'Irish Peace: a Test of Statesmanship' in June and July, and on July 24, 1919 *The Times* produced its own proposal in a unique four-column editorial. This was the establishment of two Provincial or State legislatures, one for the Province of Ulster and one for the rest of Ireland, both equally represented in the Parliament of the Irish Federation. Certain powers were reserved to the Parliament at Westminster. Thus Home Rule, partition, unity and the Imperial connection would all be safeguarded. Later, in 1920, *The Times* published an important letter from Horace Plunkett, advocating dominion status for Ireland, which was later pressed by the *Round Table*, influential in Conservative and imperial circles.

The Times served the cause of reconciliation in other ways. Steed was dedicated to Anglo-American friendship and was shocked at the bitterness which the doings of the British forces in Ireland were arousing in America; he passed on this view of things to Winston Churchill, the War Secretary. After 'Bloody Sunday' *The Times* did not content itself with deploring only the murder of the fourteen British agents; it condemned equally the attack of the Black-and-Tans on the football crowd at Croke Park, which cost twelve persons their lives.

> ... an Army already perilously undisciplined, and a police force avowedly beyond control have defiled, by heinous acts, the reputation of England; while the Government, who are trustees of that reputation, are not free from suspicion of dishonourable connivance.

Only two days before (November 20, 1920) it had published an article with an even stronger plea.

> If only the people in England knew. ... Everywhere in Ireland today you hear that cry. Why do these things happen? Why are servants of the Crown charged with pillage and arson and what amounts to lynch law, and even with drunkenness and murder? How can the reign of terror be stopped?

Later, in February 1921 it 'exploded a mine' (in the *Nation*'s words) under the government by giving details of the events which led to the resignation of General Crozier, the commander of the Auxiliaries: he had dismissed twenty-six cadets for looting, but the men went to London and saw General Tudor, Crozier's superior, who chose not to uphold him.

The *Nation's* tone was similar to *The Times'*. As early as April 1920, in an article, 'Order and Anarchy in Ireland', it declared:

> We maintain our rule . . . at a moral cost which none of us, if we were judges in another's cause, would attempt to reconcile with the general interests of civilisation.

It constantly condemned the 'atrocities' in Ireland, the 'Policy of Terror'; its correspondents gave descriptions of shootings and burnings by the Crown forces. An article 'The Guilt of the Government' stripped the veil off the troops' reprisals, and claimed that the constabulary and Auxiliaries were quite out of discipline. The shots fired at Croke Park it likened to those fired nineteen months before by British troops on an unarmed Indian crowd at Amritsar. In February 1921 it was writing of 'The loss of the British tradition'.

> Surely there is enough sense left in political England to bring this caricature of a policy to an end? . . . Is there any moral or physical evil with which Ireland in independence might conceivably threaten the British Empire worse than the injury she does us today by merely presenting the world with a picture of our existing behaviour to her?

If Ireland wanted a republic, let her have it.

Far different was the view from the right. The *Spectator* had pleaded passionately for the application of conscription to Ireland in 1918, counselling firmness and the ignoring of 'Mr. Massingham's weekly howls to the errant moon'. Its advice during the Black-and-Tan war was to enforce order by collective fines on districts where murders of police occurred: the loyal would be exempt on giving proof of loyalty, but would need to be protected, possibly in concentration camps. From fines and loyalty oaths not priests, bishops or cardinals should be exempt. After 'bloody Sunday' its article, 'The Nemesis of Murder', made no mention of Croke Park, but it girded at Asquith for denouncing the shooting of Mrs. Quinn as murder (it was homicide, the editor said). A very large number of the Southern Irish were 'uncivilized and depraved', was its comment on later murders. Its solution of the Irish question was always the same: permanent exclusion for Ulster, and let the rest of Ireland go free in complete independence: 'frankly, the history of the last two years has made us feel that the less we see or hear or know of the Southern Irish the better. . . . The ordinary Englishman has a totally different standard, moral, political and social, from that of the Southern Irishman.'

This was nothing, however, to the temper of the *National Review* and the *Morning Post*, both ultra-conservative and nationalist (the *National Review* was a monthly). The *National Review* was quite clear what ought to be done.

> Order could be restored by armed force under capable and determined men with a free hand. . . . At one time half a dozen courts-martial would have 'done the trick'; today it would probably need one hundred.

A month later (June 1920) it estimated that 1,000, 'or maybe 2,000' persons would have to be shot to attain this end; and in July it recommended General Dyer, the commander at Amritsar, as the man for the job. In August 1921, after the truce had begun, it proposed that 'Tribal Ireland', less 'Loyal Ulster', should become an independent republic, which would be far less dangerous for Britain than an Irish Dominion. The *Morning Post* was equally uncompromising. In December 1920 it denounced talk of an armistice: 'are we to have an armistice with people who murder police and manufacture bombs in cellars to blow up public buildings in their own cities?' On February 28, 1921 it wrote:

> Mr. Asquith, Sir John Simon, *The Times*, the *Westminster Gazette*, and all the other politicians and newspapers engaged in making a meal of the police in Ireland, always begin by invoking a curse upon 'Sinn Féin'. It seems to give an air of respectability to their repast. But we notice that while the fare gets hotter the curse gets shorter and more perfunctory. Thus, for example, *The Times* devoted a whole leader to the denunciation of police methods and Government policy in Ireland, but had brought the ceremonial denunciation into the space of a single phrase: 'No party in the State is in sympathy with the methods of Sinn Féin.'

None the less, it was negotiation which triumphed in the end. In the nine months preceding the truce in July 1921 the secret missions, contacts and meetings between the two sides had become almost continuous. *The Times* had its own emissaries. Archbishop Clune, Father O'Flanagan, Lord Derby, Sir James Craig, General Smuts were among the go-betweens who had some blessing from official circles, while Cope worked incessantly in the background. In June Lloyd George was told bluntly by Sir Henry Wilson that the choice was 'to go all out or to get out'. In spite of the pressure for toughness—Lord Birkenhead was declaring that Britain would never concede independence, however long the war, on the very eve of the King's visit to Belfast for his memorable appeal for conciliation —Lloyd George was pulled hard the other way. The King himself had long deplored the doings of the Black-and-Tans and had warned the government against them; Wickham Steed, Lord Stamfordham, Smuts, Edward Grigg and others concerned with the King's speech had to win round Lloyd George first; and he, with his quicksilver temperament and lack of pride, could change ground and rise to the occasion more quickly than any other leader.

If the Black-and-Tan war was a product of the coalition government, so was the Treaty. Whatever may be said about Lloyd George's methods, it is probably true that no other prime minister, and no purely Conservative or Liberal Government, could have brought the negotiations to a successful end. A Treaty in whose making Birkenhead and Austen Chamberlain took part alongside Churchill and Lloyd George could hardly be rejected by parliament. True, the Unionists threatened to make trouble during the negotiations, fearful of what pressure might be put on Ulster; a hostile motion was proposed at a party conference at Liverpool on November 17, 1921; but the efforts of Alderman Salvidge, Lord Birkenhead and others got it rejected. The *Spectator* thought that this threatened party revolt had saved Ulster: but its failure may have saved the party. Bonar Law, at that time out of office, had also warned Lloyd George not to surrender Ulster.

With the Treaty, the Irish question virtually ended for England: it divided parties and public no longer. Irish freedom was not nobly yielded, as Gladstone had tried to persuade his countrymen to yield it. It was rather that an uncomfortable, incomprehensible matter of conscience had disappeared: an awkward distraction, as Hodson, Broadbent's valet, had said in Shaw's *John Bull's Other Island* in explaining why he was a Home Ruler.

> It's because I want a little attention paid to my own country; and thet'll never be as long as your chaps are ollerin at West- minister as if nowbody mettered but your own bloomin selves. Send em back to hell or C'naught, as good ould English Cromwell said. I'm jast sick of Ireland. Let it gow. Cut the cable. . . .

For the parties the effect was more complex. In the Con- servative revolt against the coalition, which brought it down in October 1922, the Unionist resentment at the Union lost, lost after war and murder, may have played a part; the issue was kept alive in 1922 by the civil war, in which the Southern Unionists (among others) lost lives and property. But there were many causes for the unpopularity of a coalition which had held office for four appallingly difficult post-war years; Irish policy was only one, and certainly not the proximate cause of the coalition's downfall. The Conservative Government of Bonar Law made no effort to undo the settlement. Perhaps the Conservatives realized that Lloyd George had liberated them from an incubus: the Union and the Unionists. They could now turn to things more congenial to an enlarged electorate, such as widows' pensions and votes for women at 21 (it was strange that they retained the now meaningless label Unionist, as some Conservatives still do). For the Liberals the event was far less happy. With Home Rule achieved (after a fashion) and the Church of Wales disestablished, what was left for them to do? The Irish question had exhausted them, and had diverted their energies from more constructive ends in the pre-war years. The Labour Party, whose contribution to the Irish question in 1920 to 1921 had shown its growing maturity, was waiting in the wings. And in parliament there would be no more 'Irish nights': the disappearance of the Irish question made British public life a little poorer, a little more parochial.

13

EDUCATION AND LANGUAGE

By Brian Ó Cuív

FOR A COUNTRY which in the far past earned the title 'Island of Saints and Scholars' Ireland in modern times has had some singularly unfortunate educational experiences. In large measure this has been due to the alien rule which she has suffered for long centuries and which has left its mark not least in the form of the two Irish states which were created by a British Statute of 1920. Yet not all the faults and weaknesses in Irish education are due to outsiders, as we shall perhaps see from this brief survey. The 'settlement' reached in the Anglo-Irish Treaty of 1921—unsatisfactory as it may have been in many ways—did leave Ireland, North and South, in charge of much of her own affairs, including education, and it also, of course, permitted of the introduction of measures to alter the status of the Irish language and to facilitate its restoration as a vernacular. Since 1922 many differences in educational matters have appeared between North and South, but comparison between the two systems, or between either or both of them and the system in vogue for all Ireland before 1921, is far from easy, partly because of actual changes in organization and administrational methods, but also because of different methods of presentation of relevant information in official publications. To give one example, the all-Ireland Census Reports, including the last published, that for 1911, contain detailed information about education and about language. The Northern Ireland

Census Report for 1926 contains a limited amount of material on education in the county reports, but only two tables on education in the general report. In the Saorstát Éireann Census Report for the same year education was completely ignored, whereas a special volume was issued on the Irish language.

However, there is at least one obvious similarity between the North and South in educational organization. In both states the old system whereby primary, secondary and technical education were administered by separate governmental bodies has been done away with, and each has a co-ordinated department of education in charge of a minister. In fact, co-ordination had been proposed for Ireland as a whole in the Irish Education Bill of 1919 which contained the British Government's answer to the widespread dissatisfaction with the existing forms of education which had been shown for many years in the form of criticism from various quarters, including even the Boards of Education set up by the government. The bill was described in *The Irish Times* as 'The most drastic reform that has been imposed in modern times on any stereotyped system of education'. It provided for (1) co-ordination of the existing water-tight systems, (2) greatly increased parliamentary grants, (3) improved salaries and conditions for teachers, (4) a scheme of scholarships to be held in intermediate or technical schools and universities, (5) effective schemes of compulsory attendance, (6) proper maintenance of schools, (7) continuation schools for post-primary education, and (8) a scheme whereby for the first time public representatives would be given a voice in the direction of educational policy.

The Irish Times commented on the basic principles involved in the bill: 'In the first place, it recognizes that education is a single process, not a thing that can be sliced like bacon. It breaks down artificial division and proposes a system which, in operation, would establish the long-desired contact between the primary school and the university. In the next place, the bill introduces the thin end of the wedge of popular control. That feature is at once its misfortune and its chief merit: its misfortune because the measure will be opposed bitterly by influential persons in this country; its chief merit because this principle at last brings Ireland into line with the progressive democracies. The bill requires the Irish ratepayer to find money for education. That duty involves the privilege of a voice in the control of the system under which his children are educated.'

Although in matters of detail the bill had faults—and many people suspected the motives of the British Government in introducing it before a solution had been found for the political debacle in Ireland—it had several things to recommend it for consideration. Nevertheless it met with such opposition in this country, and especially from the Catholic Hierarchy, that it was withdrawn by the Government. The measure in general was described by the Hierarchy as 'an attempt on the part of the British Government to grip the mind of the people of Ireland, and form it according to its own wishes', and National Teachers were accused of 'selling their country for a mess of pottage', 'bartering the birthright of the nation', and of 'lack of loyalty to ecclesiastical superiors' because they recognized some merits in the bill and welcomed the financial proposals contained in it which were favourable to them.

The attitude of the teachers was understandable. For years they had been fighting for an improvement in their conditions of service, and this was now in sight as a result of the recommendations of the Killanin Committee which had been appointed in 1918. In fact the teachers did succeed in 1920 in making an agreement with the Treasury which secured them a reasonable salary scale, but they were not to enjoy this for long, for in 1923 the Free State Government cut the salaries by ten per cent and a cut of seven per cent became effective in Northern Ireland in 1926. As the salaries of secondary teachers were paid by the schools, and as very little money in support of them was made available from the Exchequer, their financial circumstances were even less fortunate than those of the national teachers when British rule in Ireland came to an end. But a move in the right direction in making the teaching profession more attractive to university graduates was made when the governments of the two new states introduced in 1923 and 1924 systems of incremental salaries for registered secondary teachers. The extension by the Northern Ireland Government of financial support to private elementary schools and preparatory branches of secondary schools was an enlightened action which was not followed by the Free State.

Although there was a similarity between Northern Ireland and the Free State in the matter of centralized departmental control, there were from the outset many points of difference. In the Twenty-six Counties there was no full-scale public inquiry into the whole question of elementary and superior schools, although there were some programme-planning conferences whose recommendations were important. It was not that people were satisfied with the existing systems, but it is possible that the authorities, recalling the opposition to the 1919 Bill, felt that the less changes made and the less discussion caused the better. This may explain why it is that only minor legislative items connected with education came before the Oireachtas in the form of parliamentary bills before 1926 when the School Attendance Bill was passed. Decisions taken in the department of education were put into operation either by the minister using his administrative function or by officials in their capacities as commissioners or otherwise. Thus many important issues were left without full debate, and there was a tendency to postpone reform.

On the other hand while Dáil Éireann and the Irish Republican Army were enjoying the 'breathing-space' gained by the truce negotiated in July 1921, Lord Londonderry, minister of education in the Northern Ireland Government constituted under the Government of Ireland Act of 1920, proceeded to establish a 'Departmental Committee on the Educational Services in Northern Ireland'. Although representatives of Catholic interests were among those invited to serve on it, the Catholics refused to do so. This was probably because they did not wish to appear to be accepting partition in advance of an agreed settlement between Ireland and Britain, but non-participation continued after the setting-up of the Free State. The Northern Ireland Committee's reports, completed in 1922, were followed by a comprehensive Education Act which included provision for establishing local authorities for education in Northern Ireland. This at least showed a readiness on the part of the Six-county authorities to make radical changes in a system which they had inherited and which seemed to them unsatisfactory.

For we must remember that the foundations of organized education as we know it in Ireland today were, for the most part, laid in the course of the last century. The National-School system of popular elementary education was introduced in 1831, and in spite of opposition from various quarters it expanded steadily so that by the beginning of the present century there were over 8,500 such schools with over 600,000 pupils attending them. Less than six per cent of those receiving elementary education did so in schools not under the National Board, and of that small minority almost half were attending schools run by the Irish Christian Brothers who, in fact, continued to keep their schools apart from the National Board system down to 1926, that is to the end of the period under review here. Yet in 1900 the average attendance represented only sixty-two per cent of the children of school-going age, and the rate of illiteracy at fourteen per cent was still high, though considerably reduced since 1841 when it was fifty-three per cent. It is not surprising, in view of our history, to find that the rate of illiteracy was highest among the Catholics of whom only seventy-six per cent could read and write compared with about ninety per cent of the Protestants. In many ways the majority of the people of Ireland were still suffering from the disabilities arising from alien conquest and rule. Self-government provided an opportunity of making good the deficiencies of the past, but the official approach to the problem of educational reform was very different in the two states. Because of their Unionist bias the Six-county Government have tended in the long run to follow modern educational trends in Britain, whereas in the South we have been slow to change radically from the old systems which existed under former British rule. As laid down in the Constitution the State here provides for free primary education, but beyond that it generally merely supplements private or corporate educational initiative. The Northern Act of 1923 provided among other things a basis for an expansion in whole-time post-primary education, and through further legislation this has taken place on a scale unparalleled in the Twenty-six Counties.

But perhaps the most fundamental difference in educational matters between the North and South is in relation to the Irish language, and in order to get this into proper focus we must go back far beyond 1922. When the National-School system was introduced in 1831 the majority of the children was Irish-speaking. Yet Irish was at first excluded from the schools and later only barely tolerated under very restricted conditions. In effect the whole trend of the secular side of the schooling given to Irish children was towards their assimilation in cultural and political matters by the British-minded authorities. For this and for other reasons English came to be more generally spoken as the vernacular by the people of Ireland. According to Census returns for 1891 only eight persons in every 1,000 could not speak English while 855 in every 1,000 could not speak Irish.

Had the Nationalist leaders of the nineteenth century been less occupied with political, economic and social aims, they might have given more thought to the decline of the Irish language. As it was, the National School system had been in existence for eighty years before Irish was placed on what might be considered a satisfactory footing in our schools. We all know what a difference those years have made in the magnitude of what has been accepted as a vital national task—the restoration of Irish as a vernacular. But, one may ask, how did it come about that such prominence was given to this objective when Irish had for so long ceased to be a vernacular for so large a majority of our people? The answer is to be found in the activities of the Gaelic League. The League was a vital force and its leaders had the sort of faith that moves mountains. Their object was stated clearly in the phrase 'The preservation of Irish as the national language of Ireland, and the extension of its use as a spoken language'. It was obvious that the schools must play an all-important role in the achievement of this aim. Hence the League's unrelenting agitation which brought Irish into the forefront of the educational scene. Thus in the year 1900 to 1901 they issued over 100,000 copies of eighteen pamphlets dealing mainly with education in primary and secondary schools and the universities. They badgered the Commissioners of National Education, the Intermediate Board and the university authorities. They won for children in Gaeltacht (Irish-speaking) areas the right to bilingual education in national schools and the use of the vernacular as a medium of instruction; their efforts led to a great increase in the number of English-speaking children who studied Irish in national and secondary schools; and they won the first victory for compulsion when they ensured the inclusion of Irish as a required subject for Matriculation in the newly-established National University.

It has been said that Gaelic-Leaguers of half a century ago believed that Irish would be saved and would become the language of the whole nation. That was an optimistic belief in view of the Census figures I quoted a while ago; yet when the work of the League in the schools and elsewhere began to bear fruit it seemed to many to be reasonable. But what about that sizeable minority of the people of Ireland who felt a particular allegiance to England, whose ancestors had never spoken Irish, and who feared that in a state controlled by a Catholic majority they might be victimized? It is clear from the parliamentary debates on the Home Rule Bill in 1912 that Unionists were then aware of the influence of the Gaelic League and of the possibility of compulsion with regard to Irish.

In 1913 the Ard-Fheis of the Gaelic League adopted a series of recommendations on education proposed by Eoin Mac-Neill and Seán T. Ó Ceallaigh. Included was one which said that Irish should be taught to all pupils in every National school in Ireland, and another proposed that no student be admitted to a National teachers training college unless he had a good knowledge of Irish. At the same meeting a resolution was adopted condemning John Dillon for a statement he had made in the House of Commons implying that if a policy of compulsion with regard to Irish were proposed in an Irish Parliament it would meet with such opposition from many Nationalist members that the Unionist minority would be changed to a majority on the question. The resolution put forward by the League Standing Committee was very strongly worded: 'That we regard as a grave national danger Mr.

Dillon's pronouncement on the Irish Education question ...
and that in the event of any such policy being embodied in any
future educational system in this country, we pledge ourselves
to meet it with the most strenuous and uncompromising
opposition.' It appeared that as far as the League was concerned
there would be no compromise—universal compulsory Irish
was to be the rule.

With the rise of Sinn Féin as the leading political force after
1917 the Gaelic League viewpoint became more prominent
since so many of the Sinn Féin leaders were also Gaelic-
Leaguers, some of them having come into politics via the
language movement. It is not surprising, then, that one of the
actions of the first Dáil was to establish a ministry for Irish.
Nevertheless it is hard to believe that any all-Ireland Government would have added to the possible sources of discontent
among the minority by insisting on pursuing a policy of compulsion with regard to Irish. Because of Partition the occasion
did not arise. At any rate by 1920 the League itself had adopted
a new policy for Irish which is worthy of notice. The chief
proposals for national schools were: (1) in Gaeltacht (Irish-
speaking) areas all subjects should be taught through Irish;
(2) in Breac-Ghaeltacht (partially Irish-speaking) areas Irish
should be the principal language of the school, that is, it should
be used in calling the roll, in giving orders, for prayers, etc., and
in addition a bilingual programme should be adopted wherever
possible; (3) in English-speaking areas Irish should be the
principle language as in the Breac-Ghaeltacht, and in addition
it should be taught as a spoken language for at least an hour a
day to every child in every school where there was an Irish-
speaking teacher and in every other school where a visiting
Irish teacher could be provided. It was proposed that Irish be
taught to all children in secondary schools; that in secondary
schools in the Gaeltacht it should be the medium of instruction
for other subjects; and that the authorities in all secondary
schools in other areas should be required to be ready to teach
every subject through Irish by the end of five years. Finally it
proposed that the university authorities be asked to provide
special holiday courses in subjects taught in secondary schools

with a view to these subjects being taught through Irish and an all-Irish University being achieved as soon as possible, and that no university college be allowed to confer a degree in any branch of learning on a student who could not speak Irish fluently. Although some parts of the programme were too advanced for the time, at least that proposed for national schools would have provided an excellent starting-point for the development of Irish in the school curriculum throughout most of the country. But meanwhile the Irish National Teachers Organization in their Congress at Easter 1920 decided to convene a representative conference in order 'to frame a programme, or series of programmes, in accordance with Irish ideals and conditions—due regard being given to local needs and views.' In fact the Conference was not representative, for the invitation to participate was not accepted by any of the Professors of Education in the universities or university colleges, The School Managers' Associations, The Catholic Head-masters' Association, The Christian Brothers, or The Schools Masters' Association. It was noted in the report of the Confer-ence that Rev. T. Corcoran, S.J., Professor of Education in University College, Dublin, had 'placed the benefit of his advice and experience at the disposal of the Conference', and it is likely that he had a great deal to do with the recom-mendations which emanated from it. The fact that before the Conference had completed its work the Six-county government had been set up and the Anglo-Irish Treaty ratified by Dáil Éireann may have influenced it in arriving at these recom-mendations which in other circumstances might be described as revolutionary.

The Conference's report gave as one of the most notable changes 'the raising of the status of the Irish language both as a school subject and as an instrument of instruction.' In the higher standards in the national schools Irish and English were to be obligatory subjects, but Irish was to be the medium of instruction for the History and Geography of Ireland, drill and singing. A wide range of optional subjects was proposed for higher standards, including French, Latin, Book-keeping, Rural Science and Manual Instruction. But the most radical change was to be in the infants classes. For them there was a balanced two-year programme in which Language, Drawing, Arithmetic, Singing, Kindergarten gifts and occupations would feature, but prefixed was a note: 'The work in the infants standards is to be entirely in Irish.' This was a rule which could affect nearly 250,000 children. It would, in effect, mean that the normal home language of over ninety per cent of them would be excluded from their first years of schooling. Such an exclusion of the home language had been condemned by a prominent Gaelic-Leaguer, Rev. Dr. O'Hickey, as 'an outrage upon humanity and common sense, an educational crime of the darkest dye' when the language so excluded was Irish, and Pearse had applied the phrase 'The Murder Machine' to the educational system under which it was practised. Indeed Pearse had said that he would not make Irish a compulsory subject in English-speaking areas. The rising of 1916, which so gloriously awakened the spirit of freedom in Ireland, had been described at the time in the official journal of the I.N.T.O. as a 'sad and misguided action of a not inconsiderable number of young men'. Was that rising to result in one system of repression being replaced by another on the advice of a body of educationists? The document issued by the Programme Planning Conference contains one statement which is vital in this regard. It is this: 'It was decided at an early stage of the proceedings that in the case of schools where the majority of the parents of the children object to have either Irish or English taught as an obligatory subject, their wishes should be complied with.' This provided an escape-clause for dealing with possible violent prejudices on the part of sections of the population, such as would certainly have existed in an all-Ireland state.

Leaving aside the question of the suitability in all its points of the programmes just outlined, it is obvious that it could not be brought into operation at once. Irish had not been an essential subject in the teachers training colleges, so that only native Irish speakers and the relatively small number of teachers who had learned the language could be regarded as being in any way qualified to teach it. Between 1904 and 1919 some 3,000 persons had been awarded certificates of competence in Irish after attending special courses in the Gaeltacht. But the number of teachers in national schools was more than 16,000.

Although after 1921 Sinn Féin was split by the Treaty issue there were sufficient Irish enthusiasts on both sides to ensure a forward-looking language policy in Dáil Éireann. Indeed it is likely that some members of the Treaty party were glad to give expression to their separatist leanings by means of a somewhat extreme policy on Irish, and this was made easier by the removal from its jurisdiction of the predominately anti-National North-Eastern area.

When the Free State came into being Irish was declared to be the National Language and the fight for its effective establishment as such was on. It fell to the government to make momentous decisions, for it was clear that the schools would be the principal battlefield and there was fairly general agreement that the use of Irish as the normal medium of instruction in them should be a national objective. Where there was likely to be difference of opinion was as to the best methods to be pursued to reach that objective. This was the problem that faced the government in 1922. They could decide to tackle first the immense task of providing the necessary teaching force and as a temporary measure introduce in the national schools a modified programme for Irish, such as that suggested by the Gaelic League in 1920. A large measure of success with a modified programme would have been a source of encouragement, as well as providing justification for a progressive extension of Irish in the schools. In fact the government soon made an order that from March 17, 1922 'the Irish Language be taught, or used as a medium of instruction, for not less than one full hour each day in all national schools where there was a teacher competent to teach it', but shortly afterwards the full programme of the Planning Conference was officially adopted as the basis of the national school curriculum. Reporting to the Dáil in April 1922, the minister for education said 'In regard to the Irish Language in particular more progress has been made in the last three months in the schools and elsewhere than during the whole period of the Gaelic Revival Movement.' This was indeed a surprising claim. Planning for the secondary schools had already begun and in July 1922 in the midst of civil war the first of a series of university courses for secondary teachers was given through the medium of Irish on the lines which had been suggested by the Gaelic League in 1920. A new school programme was drawn up and adopted. As in national schools, so in secondary schools Irish was to be a regular subject and was to be used as a medium of instruction as soon as possible. The first stage of the transition had been completed, and with the expected achievement of what an official of the department of education had described as 'the strengthening of the national fibre' a rapid extension of the use of Irish in all walks of life was hoped for.

In contrast to this the Northern Government did no more than tolerate the language as something to which members of the Catholic or Nationalist minority had an attachment. Outside the schools its existence was scarcely recognized officially. Within the schools, where it was permitted as an optional subject, no special effort was made to foster it and the planning of the school curricula was almost completely un-affected by it. In one respect the situation in the North was not so unsatisfactory. As a school subject Irish was classed as a modern language, attention directed towards ability to speak it, and steps soon taken to introduce an oral examination in it for secondary schools.

The years 1922 to 1926 saw in the Free State what appeared to be a logical progression from the decisions of 1922. Special emphasis was put on Irish in the teachers training colleges and in a new type of preparatory college which was intended to provide recruits for the teaching profession. Provision was made at considerable expense for the training of members of the existing body of teachers to enable them to carry out the new programme. Many of the teachers, filled with enthusiasm for the language, attended special courses and became fluent in Irish. But with others there was a tendency to concentrate on learning how to *teach* Irish rather than how to *speak* it, a fact which was to be reflected later on in the poor oral command of the language achieved by the children. A further increase in the number of adult learners came with the introduction of

Irish to the Civil Service, Army, Gárda Síochána and Law Courts. The importance of the Irish-speaking areas was not overlooked in the government plans for Irish, and in 1925 a Commission of Inquiry into the Preservation of the Gaeltacht was appointed by President Cosgrave. Its report, published in 1926, was accompanied by over eighty recommendations aimed at preserving the existing Gaeltacht areas and extending their boundaries. Possible action, and the outcome, lay in the future.

In the meantime the Gaelic League had been urging the government to take further action to strengthen the position of Irish, such as that after a period of three years no pupil who could not speak Irish reasonably well should be admitted to any secondary school in receipt of State grants. On the other hand educationists for the most part held their peace about the existing programme in the schools. In 1918 a Jesuit Father had written in *The Irish Ecclesiastical Record:* 'it is evident that when the mother-tongue is debarred from the school, nothing but educational disaster must be the result.' These words, if true for French-speaking Canada to which they referred, must also be true for Ireland; but nobody repeated them in the 'Record' in relation to the rule excluding English from all infants classes here. Could it be that Ireland was about to disprove what had been said so often about the 'Murder Machine'?

The first re-appraisal of the situation in the schools was made in 1925 by a government-appointed conference. By then it was clear that progress with Irish had been disappointing in spite of the fact that the time spent at other subjects had been considerably curtailed. The conference in seeking an explanation for this found that most of the teachers were not adequately prepared for the work which they were expected to do. As to the programme they found that it was 'open to serious objection, inasmuch as it had been framed rather to mark an ideal attainable only after lengthened and strenuous efforts on the part of educational authorities and educational bodies than to prescribe a scheme of work immediately applicable over the whole country'. Nonetheless they confirmed its most radical feature— the principle of using Irish as the sole medium of instruction for English-speaking infants. Therein, apparently, they saw 'the true and only method of establishing Irish as a vernacular'. Some words written by Davis in 1843, had they recalled them, might have led them to a different conclusion. Davis had said: 'If an attempt were made to introduce Irish, either through the national schools or courts of law, into the eastern side of the island, it would certainly fail, and the reaction might extinguish it altogether.' But the die was cast. The great experiment in converting a nation from one vernacular to another was on. It was to have a profound effect on Irish education as a whole, and only the future would tell how successful it would be.

14

DUBLIN CASTLE AND THE ROYAL IRISH CONSTABULARY (1916–1922)

By Richard Hawkins

THIS BRIEF SKETCH attempts to indicate, as a background to the events of this period, the conditions under which the Castle Government, and the police force which was its chief executive instrument, were obliged to act. The period divides roughly into what one can call 'the old régime'—up to early 1920—and 'the caretaker régime', from then on. For the Castle and the R.I.C. the first phase resembles awakening into a hangover; a period in which increasing strain shows up inflexibility of system, incapacity of personnel, inadequacy of equipment. In the second, to meet these deficiencies and the gravity of the crisis the old forms are largely replaced by executive and administrative methods based on the experience of the World War. The one phase is that of the decline of the professional; the other is the heyday of the odd-job man.

These, however, are only the last two phases in the trilogy of the Castle's downfall. The first is a period of ten to twenty years before the 1916 rising, during which both major political parties in Britain tended, with varying motives—the desire to avoid the enmity of the Irish Parliamentary Party being held in common—towards a policy of drawing the teeth of the Irish executive. The progress of this policy, only briefly reversed under Walter Long,[1] appears in such symptoms as the stopping of R.I.C. recruiting under Gerald Balfour and George Wyndham, the closing of police-stations, the termination of the Arms Act in 1906 and, as culmination, passivity in face of the Volunteer movements.[2] It is often assumed that, as neither the Castle nor the R.I.C. had altered greatly in form between the Land War and 1916, they preserved the aggressive vitality of the 1880s. In fact, the lack of change is evidence not of continued vigour but of suspended animation. Institutions such as the Viceroyalty itself, and the unpaid local magistracy, whose abolition had been considered in the stress of the 1880s, had survived, and officials unfit for active command had been left in office, because the policy imposed from London had ceased to be one which required executive efficiency in men or in system. As Home Rule seemed to be approaching, this policy of inhibition was apparently reinforced by the feeling that it was not worth trouble and money to maintain, much less improve, a machine soon to be scrapped and premises soon to be vacated. The Castle system could have been remodelled to fit its reduced role: instead, it was allowed to deteriorate, and the openness of this policy aggravated its effects by disheartening the executive personnel; especially the police, who were most

---

[1] Viscount Long, *Memories* (London: Hutchinson & Co., 1923), chap. X; and Sir Henry A. Robinson, *Memories Wise and Otherwise* (London: Cassell & Co., 1923), p. 165.

Reference to the period of running-down can be found in the memoirs of Robinson (op. cit.) his son, Sir Christopher Lynch-Robinson (*The Last of the Irish R.M.s*; London: Cassell & Co., 1951), and General Sir Nevil Macready (*Annals of an Active Life*; London: Hutchinson, 1924; vol. I, pp. 178–96), to select three sources.

[2] The closing of stations, reducing opportunities of promotion to the rank of sergeant, aroused some resentment in the Force. The Arms Act was allowed to expire against the advice of the R.M.s and Inspector-General; see the confidential memo. of James Bryce as Chief Secretary, printed for Cabinet use November 27, 1906, in the Bryce Papers, National Library of Ireland, Box 11,009–11,011, 'Irish Councils Bill' packet. For the Inspector-General's assessment of the significance of the Volunteer armies, see *Parliamentary Papers, 1916*, Cd. 8311 (xi. 185), p. 49. The fact that his warnings went largely unnoticed exemplifies the relations between government and police at this time.

directly affected. The result of suspending the action of the Home Rule Act, therefore, was that an administration and an executive, incapacitated for vigorous and effective action by years of a policy of concealed abdication, were still saddled with the responsibilities of governing. The Ulster crisis of 1914 might, if pushed to similar lengths, have demonstrated their atrophy as forcefully as that of 1916; in the interim, however, the atrophy had, if anything, advanced.

Asquith's verdict in 1916 was that the Government of Ireland had completely broken down. It is notable that the action of his government and the coalition was not to reform that system which the Commission of Inquiry on the rising called 'anomalous in quiet times, and almost unworkable in times of crisis'[1] but, firstly, to attempt to find a means of limited application of the Home Rule Act: and then to change the men at the head of the Castle Government. The rising had not been Birrell's fault—the course was set before he took the wheel, and he was unlucky to be on the bridge when rocks were struck: and it is difficult to explain why the Inspector General of the R.I.C., who had not been negligent, was replaced, unless to reassure the police that changes, possibly beneficial, would follow. This recasting of leading roles, as a substitute for rewriting, was repeated in 1918, and its effect was to accentuate the centralization of the Castle system.[2] The inexperienced Viceroy and Chief Secretary were obliged to rely upon subordinates and, responsibility being withheld from the Catholic Under-Secretary MacMahon, it fell upon the ready shoulders of Sir John Taylor, upon whom the developing emergency had already tended to push the power of decision. He was one of the few men experienced in dealing with widespread disorder and in employing the 1887 Coercion Act against it. His experience, however, like so much about the Castle and the

[1] Report of the Royal Commission on the Rebellion in Ireland (*Parliamentary Papers, 1916*, Cd. 8279, xi. 171), p. 4. This report, with the evidence taken before the Commission, provides a detailed commentary on the conduct of executive business under the Birrell régime.

[2] The following passage is based upon Mr. G. C. Duggan's 'The Last Days of Dublin Castle', printed under the nom-de-plume 'Periscope' in *Blackwood's Magazine*, vol. CCXII, August 1922.

M

R.I.C., dated from the Land War. An editorial writer in the *Constabulary Gazette* of 1918 described the Force, in terms equally suited to the entire Castle régime, as 'a wooden velocipede—a marvellous invention fifty years ago'.[1] The actions taken by the Castle under Taylor, and even later, suffered from a persistence of old forms and attitudes; Sir John consulting the Land War files and resurrecting the Divisional system of police command[2] or, with Sir Henry Robinson, attempting, through the Criminal Injuries Acts, to revive that system of financial collective punishment which had been one of the most successful coercion techniques of the nineteenth century. The need for change was admitted with reluctance: petty sessions and legal circuits which had lost their custom had to be kept up, absorbing badly needed troops and police as escorts for the officials; and the R.M.s were required to try to hobble Sinn Féin, by binding its members over on large sureties to keep the peace.[3]

A change, not of persons alone, but of outlook and method, was needed. It did not come until the spring of 1920 and the final supersession of the old Castle, after its investigation by the Fisher committee.[4] The change is somewhat ironic. Before the war, when liberal ideas and the Redmondites had influence, reform of Castle and R.I.C. had frequently been proposed, on the general lines of debureaucratizing the one and decentraliz-

[1] *Constabulary Gazette*, vol. 41, no. 2 (August 10, 1918); cf. the editorial in vol. 39, no. 7 (September 4, 1916): 'The R.I.C. may be likened unto a noble mansion of the early Victorian era, still occupied but showing visible signs of decay. . . . Over the door, in dim but discernible letters, is printed "Ichabod"—"the glory has departed".'

[2] The reintroduction of Commissioners is attributed to Taylor by Duggan (op. cit., s. III), and to General Tudor by Macready (op. cit., vol. II, p. 475). The London *Times*, however, announced their appointment on March 19, 1920, which seems to antedate General Tudor's appointment.

[3] Lynch-Robinson (op. cit., p. 167). It is fair to state that this system was used, as it had been in the Land War, as some degree of compensation for the lack of evidence to sustain prosecutions or juries to convict, and indicates a desire to use the ordinary law to the utmost extent possible. Nevertheless it seems to have been of little practical value.

[4] Macready (op. cit., vol. II, pp. 446 ff.). For a recent account of the Castle in this last phase, see John W. Wheeler-Bennett, *John Anderson, Viscount Waverley* (London: Macmillan & Co. Ltd., 1962), chap. III.

ing the other, to accord more with government and police systems in the rest of Britain. The war, however, while not originating, enormously encouraged the extension of government interference and control in Britain and the growth of semi-autonomous Boards and Departments: while nationalizing the police forces was seriously considered. The reform which came to that system which had been the model of bureaucracy was, therefore, bodily importation of the super-bureaucracy developed in wartime Britain: immense administrative staffs, headed not by professionals but by men who had supposedly demonstrated their powers of command and organization in other fields.[1] This reform affected the constabulary in particular. Of all departments the most directly involved in reasserting authority, it both needed reform and needed it more than the other departments. The new establishment absorbed numbers of English typists—the security risk of Irish staff had at last been realized—and, in positions of command, much of that surfeit of Brigadier-Generals remarked by Sir Ormonde Winter after 1918.[2] The office of Police Advisor, superseding the Inspector General and supplemented in turn by Director of Personnel and Discipline, is typical of the administrative improvisation necessary.

Events under the new régime were inevitably chaotic. Its different sections committed to policies of coercion and conciliation, it had to work with indistinct responsibilities and a scratch team, along wartime lines of trial and error, hampered by fragmentary and partial intelligence, and pressure from London which varied according to political expediency. In an alliance of such unlike policies and methods, there was source for confusion, strain and antagonism—not only between the Castle and the Imperial Government, but, within the Castle, between

[1] 'Never,' said Asquith in a public speech in 1919, 'was there a more extravagant and less successful experiment in administration.' He had become a champion of the old Civil Service against 'the men of "push and go" who had flooded the public departments under the coalition' (J. A. Spender and Cyril Asquith, *Life of Henry Herbert Asquith* . . . ; London: Hutchinson, 1932; vol. II, p. 328).

[2] Sir Ormonde Winter, *Winter's Tale* (London: Richards Press, 1955), p. 288.

those who had to fight and those who had to conciliate, and, further, between the two fighting services. Macready's command of the troops and Tudor's of the police, an arrangement intended to promote effective co-operation, resulted in an imperfect and uneasy liaison; and the co-ordination of security forces was rendered more difficult by the detachment of areas under special authorities—the southern counties under Martial Law, and the North firstly under the new Assistant Under-Secretary for Belfast, and later under the Government of Ireland Act. It was, in brief, not the old Castle which transferred power to the Provisional Government in 1922—during which transference someone burgled the Deputy Inspector General[1]—but a caretaker body installed to hold on, pending the intended abdication, to avoid the appearance of being thrown out.[2]

The predicament of the entire executive during these last seven years is epitomized by that of the R.I.C., which had, perhaps, the lion's share of difficulty. The pre-war policy of disengaging the governmental machine and neglecting its upkeep basically involved unbending the springs of action of the R.I.C.: and the Volunteer activity from 1916 onward was necessarily directed at, and bore with special weight upon, the debilitated police.

Constabulary Gazette Xmas editorials were usually sanguine. That of 1920 was an exception; that of 1916[3] was not. It looked back with pleasure on a year which had enabled the police to secure recognition of their worth, and viewed the prospect with exceptional satisfaction. We see the irony of this: but that dreary, ominous year had shone by contrast with the era of stagnation, discouragement and neglect which preceded it. The change of commanders, and the remedying of minor grievancies, seemed to indicate that reward for the men and reform in the

---

[1] Wheeler-Bennett, op. cit., p. 81n.

[2] This judgment, based on Sir William Darling's *So it looks to Me* (London: Odhams, 1952) p. 208, seems open to criticism in that it supposes a fixed intention on the part of the Imperial Government; it is not clear that anything of the kind existed.

[3] *Gazette*, vol. 39, no. 20 (December 2, 1916).

system were in train. Official policy, however, had not changed so far as to admit the need of change; Sir Joseph Byrne, who was thought of as a reforming Inspector General, expressly advised the National Convention in 1917 against any radical change;[1] and general reform came only in the overturn of 1920, when the old system would no longer work in the existing conditions. Many of the faults of that system arose from the R.I.C.'s role as an 'army of occupation'. As Tom Kettle had said, it was now an army of no occupation; but the relics of the old system continued to give trouble. It necessitated a large establishment, which made the Treasury reluctant to allow improved pay, conditions or equipment; and the dispersal of this force into localities made it difficult to deploy resources when required. At the level of district command and upward, much effort was duplicated: the amalgamation of command in the smaller counties, recommended in 1914, was not done until 1920. It was said that the basic principle of the Force was 'use two men for one man's work, and underpay both'.[2] A restrictive discipline gave scope for petty tyranny. The R.I.C. man had no recognized off-duty period, day of rest or annual leave: at night he was confined to barracks, and if single he had to live

[1] Report of the Proceedings of the Irish Convention (*Parliamentary Papers 1918*, Cd. 9019, x. 697), Appendix XV, Schedule A, p. 125. Cf. the attitude, at the 1914 R.I.C. Inquiry, of Sir David Harrel (sometime Sub-Inspector R.I.C., R.M., Chief Commissioner of D.M.P., and Under-Secretary 1893–1902), that, Home Rule being imminent, it 'was not the time for considering or suggesting reforms of an unsettling character' (Maurice Headlam, *Irish Reminiscences*; London: Robert Hale, 1947, pp. 76–80).

[2] *Gazette*, vol. 41, no. 2 (August 10, 1918). The following passage of this lecture, like the later passage dealing with morale, has been left practically unaltered and unqualified; not because it is perfect, but because there is no end to the alterations and qualifications that could be made. The 'grievances' and 'sources of discontent' which I list are distilled from repeated complaints made in the *Gazette*. The source is undoubtedly biassed, the complaints themselves possibly exaggerated and perhaps ill-founded, and their repetition probably partly due to emulation. However, they were made, and I cannot consider this fact totally insignificant. It should be noted that such complaints became much less frequent after 1919. They are not necessarily to be taken as evidence of serious grievances, nor of the general temper of the force, but of points on which discontent, whatever its origin, could focus.

there in austerity, discomfort and lack of privacy: he could marry only after seven years' service and his intended bride's character had to be approved: promotion was slow and unequal from county to county and few constables could hope to become officers: no one in the R.I.C. could vote, and there was no recognized medium within the Force for collectively negotiating reform until mid-1919, or, in practice, until the Truce. The Representative Body, having made a slow start, was hamstrung by the disruption in 1920 of the old organization and the communications system. The men had to preserve the old-fashioned 'marching order' against the unlikely possibility of its use; and regulations continued to require that an officer should own an expensive kit and a horse. Such relics of the 'military' role of the R.I.C. would have had more meaning had it been in genuine fighting trim. Its much-denounced 'military training', an abbreviated form of that given to the Regular Army, was similarly fifty years out of date and quite unrelated to the type of fighting which actually ensued, and for which experience of disorder in the North, or Western cattle drives, was no preparation. Target practice had fallen off since 1914. However, the R.I.C.'s unfitness to meet armed resistance, as shown at Ashbourne and elsewhere in 1916, did not remove its formal duty to use arms against armed rebellion, or the practical difficulty of sparing troops for the purpose. In practice and experience it was a civil force[1]: after the rising, men complained of having to carry that 'useless ornament', the carbine, rather as Roman soldiers under the late Empire refused to wear full armour. In 1919 an anxious constable asked the *Gazette*'s legal column for advice on how to act if an armed band attacked one's barracks. Should one not use the baton first and, if compelled to fire, should one not first read the Riot Act?[2]

[1] Obviously it was not so much of a civil force as a local English police force; nor, however, so military a force as the Italian Carabinieri, nor so specialized in dealing with disorder as the modern French C.R.S. It can be inferred from the *Gazette* that paramilitary work was not only unpleasant but foreign to the men. Headlam (op. cit.) considered the R.I.C. too military for ordinary police duty, but not military enough for an emergency.

[2] *Gazette*, vol. 40, no. 47 (June 21, 1919). The constable might be excused

The R.I.C. was particularly unlucky in having to take paramilitary action at a time when it was under strength by 1,200–1,500 men. While nearly 9,000 men[1] should suffice to police Ireland, the R.I.C. system of distribution needed more. Over 2,000 were in Belfast and the six-county area. The small bog-stations and dogs' nests had to be run without men enough for all the prescribed duties. When in 1918 and 1919, measures to render defensible the 1,400 barracks and huts became necessary, the three or four-man station became not only an invitation to attack but an administrative absurdity: in some, keeping all men continuously awake would not have been enough to fulfil all duties.[2] Such stations had to be abandoned; this was done with that blend of delay, inconsistency and carelessness which, for many R.I.C. men, must have seemed inseparable from any government activity. It was unfortunate that, if the force were to survive, police work[3] and the basic intelligence sources of government had to be sacrificed, and that any measure to equip it for effective action—for instance, the issue of bombs in September 1919 for barracks defence—seemed to excite public opinion. A Galway constable wrote, in late 1919, 'We have now become little moving magazines, and that familiar old adjective "semi"[-military] can easily be dispensed with in future'. It needed more than this, however, to equip the R.I.C. for a war.

Morale, chronically bad,[4] was aggravated by recent develop-

his diffidence as to the most politic course to adopt. I am informed that the rules concerning police use of weapons had recently undergone revision; and a man who fired on his own responsibility might not be supported in his action by the authorities.

[1] This figure, given in the broadcast, I find to be incorrect. In 1917 (December 5) there were 9,238 sergeants and lower ranks serving, while the total authorized strength of these ranks was 10,715 (*Proceedings of the Irish Convention*; Appendix XV, Schedule A, p. 121). The total strength of the R.I.C. does not seem to have fallen below 9,400.

[2] E.g. *Gazette*, vol. 41, no. 6 (September 6, 1919), p. 90.

[3] And other work done by the R.I.C.; legislative provision had to be made for the taking of the 1921 Census by local civil authorities (10 & 11 Geo. V, c. 42).

[4] This, again, is a distillation from the *Gazette*, and if only for that reason should be treated with scepticism. This paragraph lists some of the factors most frequently mentioned in that source as destructive of morale; and by

ments. The prospects of the force as a career had dwindled with the approach of Home Rule, which meant reduction and eventual disbandment. A force already neglected could hope for little from a native government and would lose all claim upon the Imperial Government except that of conscience; and after the war, with the treatment of ex-servicemen before them, many had little faith in the government's conscience. The prospect of good compensation was important to men who knew they would not serve out their thirty years for full pension. In a period of rising living standards police pay did not help to attract recruits or deter resignation; wartime inflation cancelled out the benefits of the pay rises of 1914 and 1916 to 1918. Men complained that the richest government in the world would not replace a uniform cap until its owner's hair grew through it. The prospects for men and even officers who left the force had contracted before 1914 and did not later improve. The unionism which disturbed the British Police at this time failed to affect the R.I.C.: it did not have sufficient *esprit de corps*.[1] Men of one rank would resist the grant of benefits to another. Older men denounced the foppish and lazy young: young men demanded compulsory retirement of the old: men suspected the officers of impeding reform. Favouritism, victimization and wire-pulling, where they did not exist, were suspected. Over all this the apparent indifference of government to the feelings, the welfare the reputation and, from 1919, the safety of the R.I.C., hung as a dark ceiling. Yet, if there was malaise in the R.I.C., it took no such demonstrative form as in the D.M.P.

In 1919, therefore, the old R.I.C. was seriously out of condition for its task. The coming of the Tans, however, needs

compression, gives them more emphasis than the original. I learn, moreover, from several sources of considerable authority, that this picture not only distorts but misrepresents the situation; and that morale in the R.I.C. was, and remained, high, despite the pressure exerted upon the men and the danger in which their families were placed.

[1] Although this reason was adduced at the time, it comes from a suspect source. It can be argued that R.I.C. discipline and distribution made agitation and organization too difficult; but they had not prevented the Limerick Police strike of 1882. The fact that there was no similar outbreak in this period is capable of more than one explanation.

further explanation. Before 1914, for obvious reasons, recruitment fell off and resignation increased gravely enough to warrant an official inquiry. They were affected, however, more by the war than by the inquiry. The Police (Emergency Provisions) Act of 1915 stopped all resignation or retirement during wartime except on grounds of health or the good of the service. Secondly, emigration was suspended: this affected the younger constables who, in peacetime, would have left to get better jobs abroad: resignation without emigration lost much of its point. Thirdly, recruitment was suspended in early 1915. The atmosphere of stagnation was thus thickened; promotion virtually halted; the one bright spot was that cadets were no longer appointed as officers. The proportion of inefficient members increased. Governmental neglect—especially toward the effects of inflation—did not make the force a better career, and it was frequently forecast that, when restrictions were lifted, old men would retire, young men would emigrate, and no one would be fool enough to join.[1] The resumption of recruiting after the rising seemed to bear this out. After an initial flow of young men, whom some suspected of hoping to dodge military service, it became clear that, even more than before 1914, neither quantity nor quality would meet requirements. In 1917 the Inspector General had to tell the National Convention that recruitment was not making good even the low wartime level of wastage. When the war did end, neither fears nor hopes were entirely realized. The force was not deprived of men; not many resigned or retired in 1919. The Inspector General, indeed, tried to encourage the inefficient to resign, and complaints that not enough did were frequent. One may suppose that the substantial pay rises of 1919, and general hopes of benefit from the Enquiry of that year, had succeeded in discouraging resignation. Recruitment, however, was as bad as before. From 1918 onward attempts were made to draw both officers and men from those who had served in the war; but demobilization, while flooding the labour market, did not make the R.I.C. a career; peace implied Home Rule and disbandment. The treatment of R.I.C. men returning from service in the forces

[1] E.g. *Gazette*, vol. 40, no. 31 (February 16, 1918), p. 521.

was inept and discouraging; men who had won commissions in the army were returned to depot as constables, and promised prior consideration for promotion to sergeant. To those with commissions, contemplating return to the R.I.C., the *Gazette* gave Punch's advice to those about to marry.[1]

It is not surprising that not enough Irish ex-servicemen joined, nor that it was decided to admit non-Irish. The state of emergency had sealed off the old source of recruits. It had also, however, reached a stage at which policemen as such were no longer strictly necessary. Recruiting in Britain may have been suggested in late 1919, when old R.I.C. were protesting that 'there is no substitute for the native Irish policeman'.[2] The appeal, at first for 1,500 men, the number by which the force was under strength, came with the new year.[3] The response was encouraging. By February rumours of lively recruits reached the men in the country, and in early March khaki-clad natives of Brighton were in Kilkenny.[4] In the crisis of 1881 to 1882 an Auxiliary Force had been formed for non-Irish and men outside the normal standards; 440 men joined in a year. From January 1, 1920 to the closing of the rolls at the end of August 1922[5] over 12,000 men enrolled, 5,000 of them in 1921. In the

[1] *Gazette*, vol. 40, no. 27 (February 1, 1919). It is of course true that however good a man's war service, he is not necessarily fitted for promotion in a police force, nor entitled to it in preference to men with continuous police service. However, if the aim was to attract men from the forces, the incentives offered were not powerful.

[2] *Gazette*, vol. 1 (New Series), no. 5 (October 18, 1919), p. 88.

[3] I do not know the exact date on which recruiting in Great Britain was opened. The R.I.C. circular of March 31, 1922 (reproduced in 'Royal Irish Constabulary: Terms of Disbandment', *Parliamentary Papers 1922*, Cd. 1618 A, xvii, p. 797) refers to men 'enlisted in Great Britain since December 1, 1919'. C. J. C. Street, in *The Administration of Ireland, 1920* (London: P. Allen & Co. Ltd., 1921), p. 277, gives January 1, 1920. The *Gazette* first discusses the matter in vol. I (New Series), no. 17 (January 10, 1920). In any case it seems not proven that Sir Hamar Greenwood, who was not Chief Secretary until the Tans were already in the country, had any hand in the decision to recruit.

[4] *Gazette*, vol. I (N.S.), no. 21 (February 7, 1920), p. 430; and no. 27 (March 20, 1920), p. 546.

[5] These figures come from the list of volumes of R.I.C. Records and Services kept by the Public Record Office, London, under the class H.O.

autumn and winter of 1920 to 1921 they were signing on at a rate of over 1,000 a month. Those approved for, and staying in, the force were much fewer; but in quantity, at least, the influx sufficed.

Some old R.I.C. had doubted the quality obtainable from the outset. British police forces, with at least equal pay and no danger, could not get recruits. No one in Britain eligible for police work needed to come to Ireland. It followed that those who did would be the rejects of Great Britain. Once again the government seemed to be seeking the easy way out, trying to achieve with numbers what required better use of existing resources. Gallipoli was frequently cited as an example of such a policy and its results. The *Gazette's* comment, that the new men were unlikely to take promotion away from the old hands, was cold comfort.[1]

The mass resignations which followed have been variously explained. Obviously, in 1920, the balance of discomfort was strongly against those who stayed in the R.I.C. The exact motives of those resigning are less easy to determine. However, in view of the ample flow of recruits, the rule which tacitly applied to the Auxiliary Division[2] probably applied to the R.I.C.—that a man who wants to resign is better out. In normal times recruits, however many and good, would not

184. The volumes relating to this period are not yet released for study, but as each contains 2,000 names, and the list gives the period covered by each volume, one can roughly deduce the number of men enlisted in a given period. Through my own error, the date August 31, 1921, was given in the broadcast instead of August 31, 1922, the final date for disbandment under the Constabulary (Ireland) Act, 1922. Recruiting in all branches of the R.I.C., having been suspended from July 10, 1921, was resumed temporarily in October to counteract wastage ('Royal Irish Constabulary, Auxiliary Division: Outline of Terms . . .', *Parliamentary Papers 1922*, Cd. 1618, xvii., p. 788; referred to below as 'Auxiliary Terms').

[1] *Gazette*, vol. I (N.S.), no 17 (January 10, 1920), upon the editorial of which the above passage is based. That it might be a case of 'rubbish to be shot here' is the *Gazette's* argument. In fact, since the job was ceasing to be a purely police job, it attracted men without police qualities.

[2] *Auxiliary Terms*, p. 2; regardless of formal contract, 'it was not thought desirable to retain in the Division Cadets who for any reason were anxious to resign'.

make up for the loss of trained men. Times, however, were not normal; given enough recruits one could use trained police sparingly as guides or instructors; draft them to where they might still be useful, or let them resign.

The tragedy of the Tan war was that the government, having allowed matters to reach a stage at which police could turn to reprisal as their only apparent means of self-defence, found it necessary to take measures which made such action more likely and more difficult to suppress. The importation of men without police discipline or inhibitions, the mass promotions, dismissals and transfers which weakened the machinery of command and discipline, were assisted by the fear that to repress the police severely would cause their utter collapse. It was thus inevitable that the reprisals should appear to receive at least the tacit consent of authority.[1] The campaign continued in the disheart-eningly slapdash style of wartime.[2] Sandbags, which rotted and kept out light and air, were not quickly replaced by steel shutters. War-surplus wireless sets, for contact between barracks instead of the vulnerable telephone, were suggested by a constable in January 1920: they were not adopted until April. Men were killed on old-fashioned foot patrols, in unfortified barracks or closed Ford vans; ex-Army holsters were issued without enough stain to blacken them, and the pay rise of 1920 brought the men into the income tax bracket. The mortifica-tions to which the Force was subjected were many and varied in degree and kind; but they contributed to a general impres-sion that the Government did not care, that it would not be

[1] That there was more to this than appearance is stated by Macready (op. cit., vol. II, p. 498) and Lynch-Robinson (op. cit., pp. 162–6); it would seem, however, that, at least at first, reprisals were spontaneous, and came to be condoned because they appeared to be effective and relieved the feelings of the security forces (Macready, vol. II, pp. 500–2).

[2] The rest of this paragraph is based upon the *Gazette*, and is therefore to be treated with the usual caution. I am told on very good authority that wireless was in fact installed, by Royal Navy personnel, in 1919; and being paid enough to bring one under income tax cannot be considered a serious grievance. However, certain actions of government were not more reassuring than the previous inaction; for instance, the Treasury sanction for the purchase of coffins for the R.I.C. at wholesale rates to secure reduction for quantity.

grateful, that it was already selling the pass behind the men who were fighting.

The *Gazette*'s hope that, with the Truce, the R.I.C. could 'resume their old protective, neighbourly and truly civic function'[1] was wishful thinking; the character of the R.I.C. committed it to paramilitary action, and its condition helped to dictate the course of events, which were such that it was almost a foregone conclusion that the Force, as it had been, would not survive whatever the outcome.

[1] *Gazette*, vol. II (N.S.), no. 31 (April 23, 1921); cf. editorials of nos. 41 and 43 (July 2 and 16, 1921).

15

THE SUMMING UP

By Desmond Williams

THE PERIOD 1922 to 1926, which ends these selected years of the 'great transition', is commonly associated with the civil war and its consequences on the general political structure of the Ireland that emerged from the Treaty. If the civil war very largely shaped the history of these years, the new Free State Government had many other affairs to deal with. While the war naturally distorted the course of events, it did not eliminate the problems of citizens going about their daily pursuits. The government, though negatively involved in military strategy, was also concerned more positively with the setting up of a new state. Objectives here covered the whole field of domestic, social and economic life.

A glance at the Dáil debates of the period will indicate the extent of political action proceeding beyond the range of military matters. The Cosgrave Cabinet, for example, introduced the following major acts: the Ministries and Secretaries Act, which determined the scope and function of the entire civil service; and the Land Purchase Act of 1923, which completed the economic revolution introduced to the countryside by Gladstone's legislation of the 1880s. Then again the courts of justice were brought into supposed harmony with Sinn Féin sentiments, sometimes in the realm of nomenclature. Here, however, the essentials of the previous judicial system were maintained. But hammering out this act and seeing it through took a lot out of men also trying to handle an armed enemy within the state. There was a good deal of legislation on the

birth and growth of a new army and police force, but their
efforts here were impeded by the armed republican enemy, and
by dissension from time to time within the government and the
Free State's own armed forces. Fiscal policy was also considered.
The chronic problem of the railways had to be faced and external relations with the British Commonwealth and the League
of Nations initiated and developed. Educational reforms were
introduced. These did not prove particularly successful, but
once again for the cabinet and its civil servants a considerable
amount of work was involved. Lastly, of course, there remained
the annual anxiety of devising budgets to meet rising state
expenditure, for the purpose of war and simultaneous peacetime reconstruction. The estimated cost of the civil war to the
state was over £7,000,000 for the first year alone, and
£10,000,000 for the following one. The foundations of the
state were laid, then, in very bad weather.

As an administrative performance, the achievements of
Cosgrave's early cabinet must rank among the more remarkable
in modern European history—rivalling in their very different
way the Adenauer régime in post-war Germany. After coming
to power in 1932 de Valera for instance, admitted he had
underestimated the amount of freedom permitted by the
treaty and by subsequent changes in British legislation affecting
the powers of the infant dominion. He also paid high tribute
to the efficiency and impartiality of the civil service which came
into being under Cosgrave's Ministry. This civil service was the
cabinet's more durable creation. Its leading members were
usually Irishmen who had worked under the British administration. They had great ability and experience, especially in the
department of Finance and the revenue commission. As with
the law courts and judiciary, method and tradition here were
British in origin. Parliamentary, legal and administrative
systems were Britain's most substantial legacy to Ireland. But a
system is useless without men to run it with courage, competence
and vigour. The new government chose its servants well, though
the origins of its purposes were often criticized. Joe McGrath,
minister of industry and commerce, for example, protested in
1924 against 'government by a clique and officialdom of the

old régime', and most of the members of McGrath's 'National Group', established after his resignation from the cabinet in the spring of 1924, left the Dáil in the following November in similar protest. Mill once wrote: 'When Society requires to be rebuilt, there is no use in attempting to rebuild it on the old plan'. There may have been in limited fields a subservient and limited following of British tradition, regarding for example, the proliferation of departments and of county council authorities.

But the old régime had a lot to be said for it. Most of its good points were taken over by the Free State. There was no real revolution in these respects, except perhaps as regards the comings and goings of personnel over the years. The British, Scottish and perhaps Rathmines went out and Mallow and Tralee came in. Indeed on occasion the civil servants embarrassed the government by their dedicated adherence to the full execution of the law; William O'Brien, for instance, as chief revenue commissioner, insisted on implementing income tax legislation in all its rigour as far as clergymen of both denominations were concerned. At the last moment this matter was discreetly disposed of by the cabinet. It was in this period that the predominance of the department of finance as a policy-influencing branch of the government was established. It aimed primarily to save the tax payer's pocket, and drew unto itself many of the ablest men in the service. Its secretary became an anonymous king. Even at that time there were those, including cabinet minister, and lesser politicians, who accused it of stereotyped parsimony. The trinity of caution, exactitude and incorruptibility proved annoying at all levels. The department's political economy may have seemed somewhat old-fashioned on occasion, and the cabinet decisively over-rode it on the Shannon Electrification Scheme. But in general its view prevailed and its fundamental scepticism of politicians seeking power and popularity at the expense of the ordinary citizen was probably quite valuable at such a stage in the country's development.

The first Cosgrave cabinet was an excellent team by any standards. It was youthful in energy, mature in judgement of the technical problems involved in developing the state's

N

authority. Cosgrave, as president of the executive council, was firm, flexible and humane. Though not as active as many of his younger colleagues, he knew how to mediate between them. His quiet dignity soon won him not only the Dáil's confidence, but widespread esteem, especially among merchants, traders, former unionists, and urban workers, as well, of course, his own Kilkenny constituents. He was rarely dragged down, even by republicans, to the arena of vehement political controversy. Republican anger was chiefly targetted at his ministers: especially Mulcahy and O'Higgins. Cosgrave was prepared to treat the opposition sometimes more gently than some colleague thought fit. He shared the doubts, for instance, of the Archbishop of Dublin and others regarding the execution of O'Connor, Mellows, McKelvey and Barratt on December 8, 1922. He sometimes avoided contentious cabinet meetings, but never went back on decision taken in his absence and defended them with proper determination. A fair comparison might be made with Attlee here regarding the essential modesty of these two men, combined with incisive intervention at critical junctures. But Cosgrave lacked the impersonal, if not inhumane approach that lent the Labour leader such command. At times Cosgrave delayed decisions, trying the patience of more impetuous ministers such as O'Higgins. He allowed Mulcahy considerable latitude in protecting and fostering the I.R.B. in 1923 and early 1924. Prudence and honest simplicity are valuable qualities for a head of government during a post-revolutionary period when stability and renovation are the guiding lights. And these qualities Cosgrave showed in high degree.

Inside the government, O'Higgins and Mulcahy were two central and opposing figures. Both were naturally involved in the civil war. On this issue their paths sometimes seemed to diverge. Each was set on seeing the war ended as soon as possible, but the differences that had appeared in the pre-civil war period re-sharpened during its conduct. Mulcahy, as minister for defence, never entirely excluded the prospects of a negotiated peace, even though any such peace would, in his view, require the acceptance of the authority of the Dáil elected in June 1922 and of the treaty. He met de Valera on September 6, 1922, without informing fellow members of the cabinet—this at a time when the Sinn Féin leader was virtually an outlaw. Towards the end of the actual fighting, in the spring and early summer of the following year, he, along with senior army officers at G.H.Q., threw out a line to selected leaders of the republican army. Mulcahy had earlier released Liam Lynch after his capture in the first week of the war, in the hope that Lynch, chief of staff of the I.R.A. would still arrange peace in the southern counties. This too he did of his own accord. But nothing came of it, and Lynch, who turned out to be one of the most active of the anti-treaty officers, was killed in action in March 1923. Tom Barry then took his place, in the General's mind, as a possible mediator.

Here, once more, enters the I.R.B. It was through this organization (virtually defunct during the civil war) that peace terms were to be negotiated and moderate republicans returned to the constitutional bosom of the Dáil. Mulcahy and the I.R.B. had formed a principal agency in the pact of May 1922. This agreement had not been acceptable to O'Higgins. Mulcahy had attended the supreme council of the I.R.B. in the week after Collins' death. General Sean McKeown, General Peadar McMahon and Gearoid O'Sullivan were also caught up with the I.R.B. (the last two being chief of staff and adjutant-general respectively of the Free State G.H.O. between 1922 and 1924). These men hoped that the secret society would not only link warriors in bitter opposition, for the purpose of using the treaty as a stepping stone to greater freedom, but also provide the nucleus of a 'national organization' designed to keep the I.R.B. out of the clutches of more extreme republicans. The old brotherhood was seemingly not yet quite dead. Though no longer an active creator of policy, its past prestige as a pressure group inside the nationalist movement could still be of use. Or so Mulcahy argued to Cosgrave and O'Higgins at an inconclusive meeting in June 1923. Here Mulcahy frankly admitted the continued presence of the I.R.B. at official head-quarters. No decisions were taken by the president and the matter was not even presented to the cabinet. At this point

O'Higgin's deep suspicions of Mulcahy's I.R.B. connections surfaced again.

Things came to a head on a far more prosaic issue in the early months of 1924. The civil war was now over and the I.R.B. had played no part in its conclusion. But the army brought together for the war had now to be demobilized. By June 1923 there were over 60,000 enrolled in its ranks. How and when were those ranks to be reduced to peacetime proportions? What officers would be dismissed, and on what terms? Here, as in the early origins of the civil war, the questions of jobs naturally arose. A conflict of interest was already apparent in the winter of 1923, rapidly mounting as the weeks went by. Another group, self-styling itself the I.R.A., led by two former associates of Michael Collins—Liam Tobin and Charles Dalton—appeared. And a mutiny broke out within the army conducted under somewhat ludicrous circumstances. An ultimatum was first sent to the president by the two officers on March 6, 1924—strange advance notice of their intention to mutiny. They denounced the I.R.B. as influencing the personnel policy on demobilization; a number of officers then absconded with amunition—mostly in outlying parts of the countryside; the rank and file in some barracks restrained other officers from promoting this conspiracy. Semi-secret meeting of the so-called mutineers took place in well-known Dublin bars and the whole thing fizzled out within a week. Ambition, one might say, should be made of sterner stuff.

There then followed a peculiar raid by G.H.Q. army officers in Parnell Square, acting under the orders of the ministry for defence. Shots were fired, by whom no one quite knew; a few men were arrested and this *petite affaire* was apparently over. Although never a serious challenge, the upheaval of this 'Day of Dupes' caused some alarm in the Dáil and among the general public. To them it was not clear whether the I.R.B. or the Tobin I.R.A. was behind it. But grumbling over jobs was really to blame. At this point, the government intervened and solved the matter by appointing an army inquiry to investigate the cause of the so called 'mutiny'. Mulcahy's senior officers at G.H.Q. were removed, whereupon he resigned. The mutineers

were eventually satisfied by the introduction of an Army
Pensions Bill. Discussions were held in parliament on the
I.R.B., around that time and O'Higgins made it clear he
personally would never tolerate the functioning of any secret
society within the army or civil service as long as he held a seat
in the cabinet. Admittedly the I.R.B. had been virtually extinct
for some time, but the old secrecy surrounding its activities
encouraged the most sinister and misleading rumours.
O'Higgins, legalist as ever, used these particular incidents to
crush it.

Now, O'Higgins and Mulcahy were both the architects of
military victory. The latter actually proposed the executions of
December 8 at a cabinet meeting, and O'Higgins (and indeed
Joe McGrath) had expressed grave doubts as to the legality or
prudence of the enterprize. Mulcahy showed ruthlessness
towards enemies of the state whenever he thought necessary;
O'Higgins tended to want the normal forms of law observed at
all times. He also thought Mulcahy had never been straight-
forward about the I.R.B. As he put it 'the minister for defence
always allowed a cloudbank to descend between himself and
the executive council'. With Mulcahy's resignation, O'Higgins
now appeared to be the guiding influence in the cabinet. This
continued until his assassination in 1927.

One other great problem confronted the Free State during
these four years. This was the outcome of the Boundary Commission, provided for in the treaty, but long delayed in assembl-
ing. By 1924 it was clear that the expectations formerly entertained by the south were vain. Public opinion in Ulster and
Britain had more or less predetermined the basic pattern of the
terms to be settled by this avowedly impartial commission. The
actual negotiations between the commissioners during the
twelve months preceeding November 25 have been discussed
elsewhere in this series. It need only be said here that the
mission of the Free State delegate, John McNeill, was hopeless
from the start. He knew this himself and had dissuaded a
younger colleague, Patrick McGilligan, from accepting nomina-
tion, for 'it will involve the political suicide of anyone who sits
on that commission'. This was a noble gesture on his part; but

was it prudent of the Free State Government to appoint such an ambassador? The British and Northern Irish Governments were kept posted of developments by their nominees; and eventually the British press was presented with a copy of the final proceedings, stolen from one of the members of the Commission. Cosgrave's Government was wholly taken by surprise. McNeill appeared not to have kept fully in touch. He certainly offered no effectively recorded challenge to the chairman's fundamental interpretation of the Treaty's provisions concerning the respective weight to be given to: (a) the wishes of the population on the one hand and (b) the economic and geographical consequences of territorial transfers.

As it was, the Commission's report was never officially published. If it had been, the Orangemen would have received more than they ever had expected. The Free State Government, fearing publication, panicked. They were only too grateful to sign an agreement with the British and Sir James Craig; in return for non-publication of the report, financial obligations under Article 5 of the treaty were cancelled and others assumed. The Border remained the same. The government would probably have had to resign if the report had appeared, but the agreement saved their faces. If they had in a way made the best of the circumstances, it was still a very poor job.

The first great crisis of the Free State since the end of the civil war had now arrived. The government had survived for the moment, but it never fully recovered from the long-term effects of this particular imbroglio.

So goes the story for those ensconced in the Dáil and related buildings. What of those who fought and lost the civil war? Soldiers started this war, not politicians. The leading soldiers set the pace, and although de Valera remained the symbol of true green republicanism, his leadership glimmered in abeyance for many months. Lynch, Toomey, Treynor, Dowling and Deasy, to take five ran the show initially. And the soldiers often grew impatient of their political leaders' reluctance to fight with no holds barred. The war in Dublin was soon over. With the surrender of the Four Courts Garrison and the death of Cathal Brugha on July 5, 1922—with guns blazing in brave,

futile demonstration—the scene of action shifted to the provinces. At first important towns in the south—Cork, Waterford,
Limerick and Tralee—fell to the republicans. But these towns
were rapidly rewon by the government, calling up their spare
gunboats. Thrust out of the towns, the republicans lost the
offensive. Hiding in the hills, they adopted the old guerrilla
tactics employed against the British. This was the second phase
of the struggle, Griffith had died on August 12 and Collins was
killed by virtual accident on August 27. Though these losses
weighed heavily on the Free State, the overall military situation
had deteriorated from the republican viewpoint. De Valera
attracted more deference. The peace talks with Mulcahy on
September 6 were abortive. So far the army had been in
absolute control of republican policy, with de Valera at the
rear. His party had no real power. On September 13, 1922,
he reviewed the situation: 'The position as I see it is this:
either (a) the Republican Party must take control, acting as the
legitimate Dáil; (b) the Army Executive take control and
assume responsibility; (c) a Joint Committee be formed to
decide policy for both.' The army was, in fact, attempting to
use de Valera as a tortoise shield, without offering him any
final say on the question of peace or war. The old conflict of the
I.R.A. and the Dáil regarding the ultimate issue of sovereignty,
(peace or war once again) was not yet resolved—even among
the republicans. Like O'Higgins, de Valera remained a con-
stitutionalist. Both distrusted army ambitions. At first de Valera
wanted his army to accept public responsibility as a government. 'The natural corollary to this is that we as a political
party should . . . resign in fact, this is the course I have long
been tempted to take myself, and were it not that my action
might prejudice the cause of the republic, I'd have taken it long
since. Our position as public representatives is impossible.'

De Valera did not resign and the republican army executive
did not take over full responsibility. Instead it declared itself
willing to render allegiance to the civil authority of a republican
government under de Valera, reserving powers in matters of
peace and war. Sisyphus, the civil leader, had his stone to roll
again—though he could rest on this point of continued ambigu-

ity until perhaps 1927 (when Fianna Fail entered the Dáil), perhaps until 1936 when he finally asserted the authority of his civil government over a gunhappy I.R.A.

What had then become the guerrilla phase of republican tactics led to mounting violence. The new policy was to disrupt civil and economic life. Bridges and railways were blown up, big houses burnt, private lives attacked. Towards the end of September 1922, the Free State Government retaliated with the introduction of far-reaching military powers, designed to meet terror with terror. Men found in the possession of arms were subject to the death penalty on that account alone. O'Higgins and Mulcahy ascribed to Erskine Childers a responsibility which he did not possess. He was a publicist, not a Machiavellian designer of economic war. The government exaggerated his role, as it did that of de Valera. In November 1922, Childers was adopted into the republican martyrology: victim of the military powers granted to the Free State Army. Cabinet ministers might have had much against him, but they were rash enough to reveal their long-standing prejudice long in advance of the emergency 'crime' for which he was 'sentenced'. This particular deterrent failed. The same cannot be said, however, of the December 8 executions, however dubious they may have been, legally speaking. These men bore a practical responsibility for civil war, which Childers did not. *Salus rei publicae, suprema lex.* Despite the dangerous implications of this doctrine the practice here at least proved effective. The policy of reprisals indicated in a republican proclamation issued on November 25, the same day on which republican government was set up for the first time, and implemented by the street shooting of Deputy Hales on December 7, was met by counter-reprisals on the part of the government. In open warfare the republicans had been defeated during the summer. As winter came on, terror was met and surmounted by more effective terror. And in the spring of 1923, the practical conclusion of hostilities was visible.

The calamity of any civil war is obvious, for the defeated, but in this case, the victors reaped no long-term benefit. If there was any change in de Valera's electoral popularity, it was to his advantage. Despite his involvement in the war, he managed in some way or other to remain above it. He was much more conservative than his Free State opponents ever supposed, and in their strangely different and contradictory fashion, Cosgrave, as leader of the Free State, and de Valera, as potential leader of the Republic, were men of middle courses. They were both constitutionalists. Both were torn between military and civil claims. And both are still alive.

The executions and the shootings separated a generation. The ill-effects of the civil war do not need elaboration. Not all the consequences were evil, for no situation is wholly evil. The civil war created a solid basis for a two-party system in the Dáil. In the long run it crystallized a parliamentary order, based on two antagonistic but reconcilable dispositions. If there was bloodshed in the south, it prevented continual sectarian slaughter in the north. Indirectly the civil war, in Anthony Eden's odd phrase about Suez, 'separated the combatants' (at least the major ones). Catholic pockets in Belfast, and blocks in Fermanagh and Tyrone could not fight alone. Perhaps this was just as well.

The possibility of clerical domination, always dangerous for the Church, was tightly checked by the survival of republicanism, conservative in politics, undenominational in national affairs (here Cosgrave and de Valera were at one) and no more disposed to accept ecclesiastical intervention in primarily political affairs than O'Connell, Tone, Parnell or John Dillon.

The civil war, and the stereotype dsituations it gave rise to, effectively killed the prospects of war between classes over the distribution of wealth. Contemporary politicians could not foresee the future in quite these ways, and would have had little patience with post-factum rationalizations of this sort. But after all 'There's a Divinity that shapes our ends, rough-hew them how we will'.